"It's Just Easier Not
to Go to School"

Joseph L. DeVitis & Linda Irwin-DeVitis

GENERAL EDITORS

Vol. 28

PETER LANG
New York • Washington, D.C./Baltimore • Bern
Frankfurt am Main • Berlin • Brussels • Vienna • Oxford

1608-01

Lori Olafson

"It's Just Easier Not to Go to School"

Adolescent Girls and Disengagement in Middle School

GUELPH HUMBER LIBRARY
205 Humber College Blvd
Toronto, ON M9W 5L7

PETER LANG
New York • Washington, D.C./Baltimore • Bern
Frankfurt am Main • Berlin • Brussels • Vienna • Oxford

Library of Congress Cataloging-in-Publication Data

Olafson, Lori.
"It's just easier not to go to school": adolescent girls
and disengagement in middle school / Lori Olafson.
p. cm. — (Adolescent cultures, school, and society; v. 28)
Includes bibliographical references.
1. Teenage girls—Education (Secondary)—Social aspects—United States.
2. Middle school students—Social conditions—United States.
3. Body image in adolescence—Social aspects—United States.
4. Body image in women—Social aspects—United States.
5. Feminism and education—United States. I. Title.
II. Series: Adolescent cultures, school & society; v. 28.
LC1755.O53   373.1822—dc22   2004014183
ISBN 0-8204-6762-6
ISSN 1091-1464

Bibliographic information published by **Die Deutsche Bibliothek.**
Die Deutsche Bibliothek lists this publication in the "Deutsche
Nationalbibliografie"; detailed bibliographic data is available
on the Internet at http://dnb.ddb.de/.

Cover design by Sophie Boorsch Appel

The paper in this book meets the guidelines for permanence and durability
of the Committee on Production Guidelines for Book Longevity
of the Council of Library Resources.

© 2006 Peter Lang Publishing, Inc., New York
29 Broadway, New York, NY 10006
www.peterlang.com

All rights reserved.
Reprint or reproduction, even partially, in all forms such as microfilm,
xerography, microfiche, microcard, and offset strictly prohibited.

Printed in the United States of America

For Rob and Gregg

Contents

Preface

· ·

It is important to admit that we study things that trouble or intrigue us, beginning from our own subjective standpoints. (Hertz, 1997)

Feminist researchers frequently start with an issue that bothers them personally. (Reinharz, 1992)

IN 1997, A GROUP OF PEOPLE CONSISTING OF A SCHOOL PSYCHOLO-gist, a school administrator, classroom teachers and two research-ers (including me) identified a 12-year-old girl, Diane, as at-risk for school failure. Diane exhibited many of the early warning signs of what is typically considered resistance to schooling: poor attendance, refusal to complete school assignments, and skipping classes (Kohl, 1994; Sun, 1995; Willis, 1977). For this reason, Diane and her parents were asked to volunteer for a research project called "Understanding and Educating Resisting Students." In their grade seven year, Diane and five other students were part of a collaborative research effort between a middle school, a school division, and a large university located in western Canada. One of our stated research goals was to improve academic success for these students and to decrease their potential for dropping out of school. Over the course of the year, Diane's school achievement and her report card grades improved. She discovered that "it was just stupid not to do work" (03/10/98).

Unfortunately, funding to continue research at the classroom level was not obtained, and the participants were distributed amongst different classrooms for eighth grade. Diane had also consented to participate in my dissertation study, so our conversations continued into her grade eight year. When I was interviewing at the school in January 1999, I mentioned to another participant that I wanted to interview Diane again. I was informed that Diane had dropped out of school.

This turn of events was more than "troubling" or "intriguing" or personally "bothersome." A child who had been identified by school staff and researchers as at-risk for school failure, and who had participated in a research project that was intended to prevent students from dropping out, had somehow managed to slip through the cracks and quietly vanish. When I contacted Diane by telephone at her home, she was adamant about not returning to school. According to Diane, none of the teachers cared anyway (01/21/99).

This incident, occurring near the end of my time in the field, characterizes what I found to be common themes in the lives of adolescent girls: disengagement from school, the complexity of peer relationships, the absence of caring relationships between students and teachers, and the inability of adults in the school to respond sensitively to individual students. Throughout my teaching career, I recalled hearing similar themes as those expressed by the participants in this study, and incidents such as Diane's school-leaving seemed to happen far too frequently. The title of the book ("It's just easier not to go to school") is a comment from one of the girls in the study that is reflective of their experience of schooling. This book is my attempt to understand and describe the conditions of schooling that create the difficulties and struggles of life in school for adolescent girls.

one

Introduction

· ·

THE PHENOMENON OF RESISTANCE IS COMPELLING, COMPLEX and more than troubling. It is a phenomenon that has intrigued me for many years. I have not been, however, "the paragon who always knows the Right Way and executes it flawlessly" (Becker, 1986, p. 67). Rather, the remainder of this chapter that describes my orientation to the phenomenon of resistance takes the form of what Becker calls a "Confessional Tale" by admitting to the troubles that I have had along the way.

Orientation to the Phenomenon

In 1995, the first paper I wrote regarding the phenomenon of resistance was entitled "School Sucks: Marginalization, Opposition, Counter-School Culture and School Failure." This paper told the story of Ernest, a high school student who had experienced, and was continuing to experience, school failure. Ernest had been retained in grade seven and had failed English, Math, and Science in grade ten. He rejected the school work and opposed the authority of teachers:

"I didn't listen to the teachers, mouthed them off, didn't do work, didn't listen or do what they said. I told them what I felt and they didn't like that either" (Interview: 07/14/95). In grade eleven, Ernest dropped out of school.

I continued a formal study of the phenomenon of resistance for my thesis. This study was originally titled "Assessment of Marginalized Students." I decided to focus on classroom assessment because I felt that for Ernest, the methods by which he had been assessed had contributed to his school failure. Classroom assessment, according to Stiggins (2001), is the development and delivery of accurate information about student achievement using a variety of assessment methods. But the classroom assessment of marginalized students like Ernest can be particularly problematic because marginalized students, like "the lads" in Willis's (1977) study, struggle to win space from the institution and its rule by not working. When students resist doing the "work" they receive failing grades. I believed that traditional assessment and reporting procedures contributed to and perpetuated the marginalization of these students, and through my research I hoped to uncover alternative practices for the assessment of marginalized students.

However, the final title of my thesis, "Rejecting the 'Docile Body': Resisting Students and the Regime of Truth," signaled major theoretical shifts that occurred as I engaged in the research. For example, I used the term "resist*ing*" students instead of "marginal*ized*" students, recognizing that the participants in the study were actively rejecting certain institutional beliefs and practices and were not simply passive recipients of oppression. The final title does not contain the word "assessment," representing a change in focus from the tools and methods of assessment. In the interviews, the students did not discuss at length the methods and tools by which they were assessed. Instead, they emphasized the social, personal, and interpretive features of assessment. Particularly compelling as a social feature of assessment was the nature of the teacher-student relationship and its effect on student behavior and achievement. The students in this study felt that a positive teacher-student relationship improved their performance: "It's the teacher that you get that changes how well you do" (Olafson, 1996). I argued that assessment systems are used as a means for maintaining institutional control, they perpetuate asymmetrical power relations, they are taken for granted, and they are a key message system for promoting the single truth of the dominant school culture.

This research study was the genesis for a collaborative research project between me, the university, a school district, and a middle school. This study, "Understanding and Educating Resisting Students," occurred during the 1997-98 school year. The project consisted of two interrelated phases, one based on coming to know the phenomenon and the other on designing and enacting curriculum and assessment practices in the grade seven classroom in which the participants were situated. The results from this study indicated that resistance is not always located in particular individuals or in particular places, and that the notion of resistance is slippery and discomforting. The instances would not "sit still" in the analytic categories that we developed (Field & Olafson, 1998). In developing and enacting the curriculum in the classroom, we found that some of the instructional strategies worked some of the time for some of the participants, and that what worked in one instance for a particular student was not necessarily successful in other instances or on other days. An insight from this study, the appearance of what I believed to be gendered forms of resistance, prompted my desire to focus additional research on the experience of resistance for middle school girls.

At the beginning of this research, I was interested in the phenomenon of becoming and being resistant as experienced by adolescent females. The original research question was "For the participants, what is the experience of resistance like?" But as the study progressed, it became less about resistance to schooling than about the conditions of life in school that led to disengagement.

As I conducted my research I found ample evidence that what has become commonly known as the contemporary crisis of female adolescence (Brumberg, 1997; Gilligan, Lyons & Hanmer, 1990; Pipher, 1994; Sadker & Sadker, 1994; Taylor, Gilligan & Sullivan, 1995) was flourishing at the site of the school. This "crisis" has a historical foundation according to Brumberg (1997): at the end of the twentieth century, living in a girl's body is more complicated than it was a century ago because prior to the twentieth century, "girls simply did not organize their thinking about themselves around their bodies"

(p. 97). Many girls today believe that the body is the ultimate expression of self (Brumberg, 1997). At the research sites, participants' talk often focused on the body. They were overwhelmingly concerned with the appearance of their bodies, and their body talk compelled me to explore the concept of the body as a frame from which I could begin to interpret the significant events in their lives. Another topic participants frequently discussed revolved around the complex web of social relationships that they constructed and by which they were constrained in the context of their schooling. What emerged, then, was a picture of the school as a social world and as a place of conflicting desires, identities and bodies. The phenomenon of resistance was but a part of this social world.

The Struggle for Meaning

> The published text represents only a fraction of the struggle for meaning which accompanies its production. (Gore, 1993)

The struggle for meaning began long before I began to produce text. As the focus of the study changed from identifying and interpreting various kinds of resistance in adolescent girls, I experienced the struggle as a tension between doing what I had set out to do versus investigating what seemed to be a more compelling phenomenon. Certainly, talking about the experience of resistance led to the emergence of themes that centered on the body and the social world. Had I not begun by talking to the participants about instances of resistance, this study would not have evolved as it did.

I struggled also with language. As Belsey (1980) notes, "it is only within language that the production of meaning is possible, however much of our individual experience of producing meaning is one of tumbling and panic, and of looking for adequate formulations of what seems intuitive" (p. 25). In my struggle with language, I also experienced what Becker (1986) calls the compromise between conflicting possibilities. Inherent in any text, including those jointly produced by me and the participants, are a range of possibilities of meanings (Belsey, 1980). I chose to use primarily feminist and poststructural theories to interpret the meaning participants gave to their own lives. This work is grounded philosophically in the work of Foucault and empirically in the life-world of adolescent girls at school. While this framework opened what I felt to be a fascinating world of female adolescence, it also undoubtedly closed off possible alternative interpretations.

In addition to the struggle for meaning, I also experienced a struggle for structure. The structure emerged only as I textually progressed with the work (van Manen, 1990). My main concern was that I structure the writing in such a way as to avoid the "tyranny of lucidity" (Belsey, 1980) and the impression that I have yielded to what Gore (1993) calls the modernist temptation for universal explanations and solutions. From the struggles for meaning and for structure, my hope is that a text has emerged that embodies the spirit of interpretive research, a text that presents information that disrupts conventional thinking, challenges taken-for-granted thinking about power relationships at school, and demonstrates a commitment to understanding context without reducing particularity (Eisenhart, 1998). In writing this book I attempt to foreground the participants' narratives. By attending to the multiplicities of particular contexts (a middle school and a junior high school), I provide what Gore (1993) calls phenomenological accounts of multiplicity and contradiction within each chapter.

In chapter 2, the conditions and circumstances of the study are described. This chapter provides the who, what and where of the research by providing descriptions of the research sites, the participants, and the research activities. These descriptions include an account of the transformations that occurred—that is, how the research evolved from describing the different kinds and forms of resistance to the inclusion of new topics and themes that arose from the interviews. The key tensions that arose in the field are also included. I use Reinharz's (1997) notion of brought and created selves in the field as a frame to describe the methodological and ethical dilemmas I encountered. This section moves beyond the traditional discussion of dilemmas that focuses on the roles of participant-observer and interviewer.

In chapter 3, I demonstrate that generally accepted conceptualizations of resistance gloss over rather than reveal a more thoughtful understanding of the topic (van Manen, 1990). Using the participants' narratives, I "counter dominant discourses by providing actual accounts of classroom situations that put into question broad-er theories" (Gore, 1993, p. 48). The broader theories of resistance from both critical theorist/Marxist and poststructural perspectives are undermined by identifying multiple meanings of resistance and possibilities for resistance that are not accounted for by these theo-ries. In this chapter, then, the literature on resistance is embedded within an analytic approach that uses relevant anecdotes to show how a particular phenomenon is ill understood (van Manen, 1990). Chapter 3 concludes with a discussion of Foucault's conception of resistance, one that I believe is useful because it makes possible the identification of what Nicholson (1999) calls multiple meanings in the present.

Chapter 4 describes the process of thematic analysis that resulted in reconstructed life stories for each of the participants. Reconstruct-ed life stories are an attempt to uncover and describe the structures of lived experience that include an analysis of what was most com-mon to the experience (van Manen, 1990). Two reconstructed life stories are presented in this chapter that illustrate the three general themes found within all the reconstructed life stories.

In chapter 5, I describe how I use insights from the work of Fou-cault as theoretical lenses through which to view the three general themes as they relate to constituting bodies and subjectivities in ado-lescent girls. I do not provide a detailed critique of Foucault's work, which is not to say that I have uncritically accepted the totality of his work. Rather, I have appropriated what I found to be useful. I have taken quite literally the words of Foucault as he encouraged the ap-propriation of his ideas by saying, "If one or two of these 'gadgets' of approach or method that I've tried to employ… can be of service to you, then I shall be delighted" (1980, p. 65). The appropriation of useful Foucauldian concepts is not unheard of in feminist work. As Hekman (1996) states, "feminists are under no compulsion to accept the totality of any theorist's work. Rather, we can and should appropriate aspects of a particular body of work that suit feminist purposes" (p. 9). The aspects of Foucault's work that suit my femi-nist purposes for this study include the concepts of regime of truth and relational power.

I acknowledge certain limitations of Foucault's work. Some of these limitations are responded to within the structure and content of the text. For example, Foucault was not interested in what individuals had to say, especially girls and women. I see this as a limitation to Foucault's work, but it is not one that occurs in my own work as I deliberately focus on the specific struggles of particular adolescent girls. In this way, I am responding to Hartsock's (1990) criticism of Foucault's "vagueness" and to what Roman (1996) calls the responsibility to rework the many oversights of gender in masculinist thought. Foucault, after all, is "yet one more androcentric European male theorist" (Hekman, 1996, p. 1). Another criticism directed at Foucault's work is that he treated the body as if it were one, "as if the bodily experiences of men and women did not differ" (Bartky, 1990, p. 65). Again, this limitation is directly addressed in my work by using the concept of regimes of the body to discuss the bodily experiences of adolescent girls.

Many educational theorists have pointed to the ways in which schooling practices discipline the body (Kelly, 1997). The focus of this work has been on describing how institutional power regulates and disciplines what Foucault calls the "docile body." In chapter 6, I use insights from this work, showing that the official practices of schooling do indeed discipline the body, producing subjectivities of particular types. I refer to this set of discourses and practices as an institutional regime of the body. The dominant school culture is one regime of truth that is actualized at the level of the classroom, and it is resistance to relations of power in this regime that much of the previous research (including my own) is concerned with. However, this "official" regime is by no means the only regime experienced by students. The school is a site where multiple regimes of truth operate. In addition to the institutional regime, students are subject to cultural regimes (for example, the dominant model of femininity) and to regimes they have socially constructed themselves through what Finders (1997) calls the "power of the peer dynamic." According to Gore (1993), regime of truth can be applied to discourses and practices that reveal sufficient regularity: I use the participants' narratives to identify specific practices that occur with regularity within the multiple regimes. At the school, then, there are multiple and competing regimes of truth. I show how specific practices in each regime discipline the participants' bodies (individually and collectively) in particular ways.

In chapter 7, the school gymnasium is described as a location that reveals specific practices from multiple regimes operating simultaneously. Not only is the body schooled through the use of institutional power, it is also schooled culturally and socially within physical education classes. These practices range from the institutional regime's attempts to regulate and to assess the movement of the body to practices of the student-constructed regime (mocking as a practice of exclusion). I view physical education as a site of struggle for the young women in this study, a site that is chiefly about the struggle for identity. In the discussion of identity, I introduce the psychoanalytic perspective that desire is a key component in the struggle for identity. Regimes of the body attempt to structure the desires of subjects in particular ways in order to produce particular forms of subjectivity. The participants in this study accepted, desired, challenged, and refused subject positions that were suggested and imposed by various regimes of the body. In this chapter I come to understand that resistance is primarily resistance to particular subject positions.

In chapter 8, as I began to consider the implications of the study, I recognized another limitation of Foucault's work: the analytical tools provided by Foucault (regime of truth, relational power) that unmasked some of the hidden workings of power were not sufficient for the kind of moral imagining that I believe is necessary to address the questions of how teachers and students can try to go on together in shared terms (Walker, 1998). Consequently, I advocate the use of the expressive-collaborative model of moral understanding (Walker, 1998) as a means to reframe and explore possible resolutions to the "problems" of adolescence, and I suggest revisioning the teacher-student relationship from its current state as a bureaucratized relationship (Davidson, 1996). This move toward conversation, listening, and understanding represents an interpretive turn—a move away from Foucault in order to engage in moral imagining.

I begin to articulate possible pedagogical interventions from the standpoint of a feminist educator, recognizing, of course, that feminist pedagogy is itself a regime of truth and that "everything is dangerous" (Foucault, 1982b). With these cautionary notes in mind, I return to physical education to consider how specific practices that "unsettle girls' sense of Self" (Currie, 1999, p. 209) might be revisioned in order to provide girls with a space in which to begin to develop a critical stance to the ways in which their bodies have been constructed.

two

A More Complete Telling

M̲Y RESEARCH INVOLVED 10 GIRLS IN GRADES SEVEN AND EIGHT who attended 2 different schools, one a middle school with a grade five through eight configuration, and the other a junior high (grades seven through nine). The title for this chapter comes from Hertz's (1997) call for a more complete telling of the research process: "through personal accounting, researchers must become more aware of how their own positions and interests are imposed at all stages of the research process—from the questions they ask to those they ignore, from who they study and who they ignore, from problem formation to analysis, representation, and writing" (p. ix). In this chapter, I describe the participants, the context in which the study was undertaken, and the what and where of the research activities.

To begin with, I was interested in adolescent girls in grades seven and eight and the ways in which they made sense of the experience of resistance to schooling. My intention was to develop a more complex understanding of resistance by identifying the conditions that give rise to resistance and by describing the different kinds and forms of resistance. Very quickly, though, the research took an interpretive turn that I felt obliged to follow. The participants were eager to share stories of their experiences of schooling, but in addition to their stories of resistance, they spoke repeatedly of the complex web of social relationships that they constructed, and were constrained by, in the context of their schooling. Their negotiation through these webs involved intricate and complicated strategies, and resistance, not only towards schooling, was very often a response to a variety of different social relationships. As a part of the "more complete telling" of the research process, I attempt to provide in this chapter an accounting of the ways the research emerged.

Tradition of Inquiry

Creswell (1998) outlines five traditions of inquiry that are found in qualitative inquiry. The methodology of the current study was guided by a phenomenological approach to inquiry. Broadly speaking, a phenomenological approach is primarily concerned with attempting to understand the meaning of events and interactions from participant perspectives (Bogdan & Biklen, 2003). In the case of the current study, the attempt was to understand how the girls interpreted their lives at school, paying particular attention to the specific experiences that led to their interpretations. Specifically, the study can be viewed as hermeneutic phenomenological research in that it is descriptive and interpretive; that is, the facts of the girls' lived experiences are meaningfully experienced and interpreted by themselves and by the researcher as they describe their experiences (van Manen, 1990).

According to van Manen (1990, p. 30–31), the methodological structure of hermeneutic phenomenological inquiry is seen as a dynamic interplay among six research activities:

1. turning to a phenomenon which seriously interests us,
2. investigating lived experience,
3. reflecting on the essential themes that characterize a phenomenon,
4. describing the phenomenon in writing,
5. maintaining a strong and oriented relation to the phenomenon, and

6. balancing the research context by considering parts and whole

In the next section of the chapter, the research activities are described. As noted, by van Manen (1990), phenomenological research takes its point of departure from the empirical world. The details of the empirical world of the current study are thus provided in the following descriptions of the research sites, participants, and data collection activities.

Research Sites

The research was conducted in two classrooms at two different schools located within separate school divisions. The school sites, participants, and individual teachers are identified by pseudonyms throughout this study. The two sites were chosen because of established connections, a common rationale: "It seems quite typical for outside researchers to gain access to settings or persons through contacts they have already established" (Lofland & Lofland, 1995, p. 38). At first glance, it appeared that these schools had very little in common. Creekwood Middle School was a new school located in a middle to upper-middle class subdivision of a small town near a large city in western Canada. The school had little ethnic diversity, and the majority of students were Caucasian and English-speaking. The other site, Kingwood Junior High, was located in a major urban area 42 kilometers from Creekwood Middle School. This school, aged, crumbling, and filled with graffiti, was in a low socio-economic neighborhood of the city. It had a reputation as a "tough" school. There was a high English-as-a-Second-Language population, and many of the students were recent immigrants. As I immersed myself in the fieldwork and interviewing, it became clear that common themes arose from both sites.

I experienced simultaneous advantages and drawbacks at each site. At Creekwood, I was funded through the "Understanding and Educating Resisting Students" research project to provide part-time support to a grade seven class. Previously, I had been employed as a classroom teacher at the site. Employment at the fieldwork site has occurred previously in feminist research and can be one way of minimizing the distinction of the researcher role (Reinharz, 1992). My prior involvement at the school, both as a teacher and as researcher, was both an advantage and a drawback. I had an intimate knowledge of the school, its organization, its administration, its teachers, and its students. I knew how to access student records, and I moved freely about the school, talking informally with teachers and students. Whenever I requested interviews with particular students, the teachers granted permission. In many ways, I was an insider. However, this position also had many drawbacks. Although I established rapport with many of the students, the participants and I had difficulty breaking out of a teacher-student relationship. Instead of listening, I wanted to assume a teacher perspective and admonish them for not doing their homework or skipping classes. I knew many of the staff members personally and professionally, and it was difficult to set these relationships aside as students related stories about their teachers—teachers who hated kids, teachers who didn't adequately prepare lessons or insisted on completion of tedious activities, teachers who called them names and punished them for breaking a multitude of rules.

Mr. Kim, a teacher at Kingwood Junior High was a fellow graduate student who volunteered his grade eight classroom as a second site. This classroom consisted of 40 students, two teachers and one teacher assistant. These students had been grouped together because of their demonstrated low achievement at the school. Many of them had repeated grades in elementary school, and several had recently failed their grade seven year. Fifteen students were identified as learning disabled, and the remaining students had difficulty with work completion and organizational skills. In this setting, I was much more of an outsider and more time was required to build rapport with the students before I asked for volunteers to participate in the research. I visited this classroom weekly for five months prior to interviewing. The research advantage in this classroom was that students did not view me as a teacher, and I was able to notice more of the underlife of the classroom, or those activities and comments that are meant to be hidden from teachers.

The data collection at both sites, each with their advantages and drawbacks, mutually informed the direction of the research, generating topics and questions beyond those I had originally envisioned.

For example, when I became aware of the nature of the underlife in the classroom at Kingwood I became more attentive to the underlife at Creekwood. When common themes, such as acceptance and popularity, were expressed by both sets of participants in the interviews, I focused subsequent interviews and fieldwork on further understanding these themes. I often checked the experiences and interpretations from participants at one site with the participants from the other site, asking questions such as "I've heard that a big part of being popular has to do with your looks. Is that how it works at this school?" Collecting data at two separate sites allowed me to see that the girls had similar concerns about their lives at school that transcended the differences in geographical location and economic status.

Participants

I was interested in girls who were reported to experience chronic problems in school—who were competent and able but willfully unsuccessful at school. At both sites, I enlisted teacher support for identifying resisting students by discussing characteristics and specific behaviors associated with resistance. Teachers were provided with a checklist of resistant behaviors and were asked to refer students who fit the profile. Specifically, teachers were asked to identify students who demonstrated:

- Discrepancy between ability and achievement
- School failure (e.g., report card grades of "D" and "F")
- Willed not learning (Kohl, 1994) evidenced by incomplete assignments and homework or inattention in class
- Symbolic and physical withdrawal (lateness and non-attendance of school or particular classes)
- Opposition to authority (Willis, 1977), including confrontational relationships with school staff
- Lack of respect for school rules and regulations (Sefa Dei, Massuca, McIsaac, & Zine, 1997), such as damaging school property, and breaking school rules
- Acts of defiance (e.g., fighting, swearing, or other behaviors requiring administrative intervention).

Creekwood Participants

The six participants at Creekwood were in seventh grade in the same classroom. All were Caucasian and, I suspect, middle class although I did not confirm this. I asked the three girls participating in the "Understanding and Educating Resisting Students" study at Creekwood School to participate in my research. Raye, Dianne, and Alicia, already identified as resistant for the purposes of the "Understanding and Educating Resisting Students" study, agreed to participate. Consent forms were sent to the parents. Parents were informed that I would be interviewing, accessing their daughters' cumulative records and confidential files, and collecting samples of school work. Additionally, parents were informed that their daughters had been asked to volunteer for the study because they had experienced difficulty in school subjects and/or their learning interactions. Participants also completed a consent form.

As I developed a more complex understanding of resistance, I expanded the study to include participants who were not overtly resistant to schooling but who engaged in more subtle forms of resistance. Based on my observations in the classroom, I asked three more girls at Creekwood (Angela, Rebecca, and Brenda) to participate, and again consent forms were sent to parents and participants. In addition to being informed of the data-collection activities, parents were informed that their daughters had been asked to participate because they were "able to articulate many of the issues encountered by girls as they negotiate the difficult terrain of adolescence at school."

Kingwood Participants

At Kingwood Junior High, after spending five months as a participant-observer in Mr. Kim's eighth grade classroom, I spoke to the girls as a whole group, requesting volunteers for the study. All of the girls expressed interest, and each student was given a consent form. It seemed, as Holstein & Gubrium (1995) maintain, that the mere invitation to participate was sufficient incitement for these potential participants. These students received the consent forms that informed their parents they were being asked to participate because they had experienced difficulty in their school subjects and/or learning interactions. Two weeks later, Mr. Kim assured me that the girls wanted to participate, but consent forms had not yet been returned.

He continued to encourage the girls to return their forms and spoke privately to girls whom he felt would be a good addition to the study based on the identifying characteristics we had discussed. Finally, I received consents from four students (August, Emma, Sheresa, and Lynn), bringing to ten the number of participants for this study. As with the participants at Creekwood, the four girls at Kingwood were Caucasian. However, unlike the Creekwood girls, I suspected that the Kingwood girls were not middle class because the school was located in a working-class neighborhood and from information provided by the girls. Lynn, for example, volunteered that her father had been laid off and that at times there was not sufficient food in the house.

At each site, I strove for openness and empathy with the participants and not the superficial friendliness of which Reinharz (1992) warns. I was able to build close relationships with the girls, primarily because they viewed me as someone who would spend time talking with them. I asked one of the participants why she was always so eager to be interviewed—was this simply a great way to miss class? She replied, "No, you're good to talk to. No one else will listen" (Field notes: 06/15/98). Without exception, the girls were always willing to be interviewed, and they often initiated interviews. At the end of an interview, one participant remarked, "When can we meet again? I have so much to tell you" (Field notes: 05/11/98).

Data Collection

Approaches, or techniques, for collecting lived experience material included observations, interviewing, and collecting school documents and artifacts produced by the girls. Participant observation and intensive interviewing are interrelated methods that are often combined (Lofland & Lofland, 1995), especially in feminist work (Reinharz, 1992). From a feminist perspective, fieldwork makes women's lives visible and interviewing makes women's voices audible (Reinharz, 1992). The combination of participant-observation and interviewing allowed me to make the lives of the girls both visible and audible.

The third component of the research method was document analysis of cultural artifacts that were produced at the school sites. These artifacts, produced by the participants and by the institution, added another layer of meaning beyond what the girls actually said and did.

Interviewing

Multiple, in-depth interviewing of the participants, also known as phenomenological (van Manen, 1990), feminist (Reinharz, 1992), or intensive interviewing (Lofland & Lofland 1995), was the primary data-collection activity. The purpose of such interviewing is a means for exploring and gathering experiential narrative material (van Manen, 1990). The assets of multiple interviews include the potential for developing trust by helping to form the strong interviewer-interviewee bonds characteristic of feminist research, and the opportunity to share interview transcripts with the interviewees (Reinharz, 1992). Interviews at the Creekwood site began in January 1998 and were intended to conclude at the end of the school year, June 1998. However, due to my continued part-time employment at the school, I continued my relationship with the girls throughout the 1998-1999 school year, conducting follow-up interviews until March 1999. In addition to these interviews, I also spoke informally with the girls in the hallways, lunch room and office at the school. They regularly approached me at the school in order to provide updates on the shifting social scene at Creekwood.

The interviews at Kingwood Junior High concluded in June 1998. When I realized that I would continue interviewing at Creekwood, I also considered resuming interviewing at Kingwood. Unfortunately, Mr. Kim had transferred to another school, and three of the four participants were no longer attending Kingwood. Two students had moved to an alternative program at another school, and the third student was re-admitted to the school from which she had previously been expelled. For these reasons, I did not attempt to locate and interview the Kingwood participants.

In the interviewing process, I made the assumption that the participants were competent narrators of their lives (Holstein & Gubrium, 1995) and that "the way people talk about their lives is of significance, [that] the language they use and the connections they make reveal the world that they see and in which they act" (Gilligan, 1982, p. 2). While I doubted at times the factual content of their narrations ("The teacher called me a 'bad ass'"), I considered their voices to portray the world they saw and in which they acted. With the exception of one participant, August, I assumed a stance of trust rather than suspicion. According to Reinharz (1992), "a feminist researcher should begin a research project intending to believe the interviewee and should question the interviewee if she begins not to believe her" (p. 29). I began to disbelieve August's narratives when they became infused with celebrities; for example, on one occasion, August informed me that a singing group (the Back Street Boys) had been contacting her regularly. In this instance, I checked August's account with Mr. Kim, as I was perplexed by her insistence that an internationally acclaimed music group was telephoning her. According to Mr. Kim, August often came up with what he termed "wild" stories: "she's certainly a storyteller. I'm not sure whether she's making them up or if she truly is delusional" (Interview: 06/24/98). From that point, I regarded August's stories with suspicion.

With the exception of August, then, I believed the participants' accounts. I also recognized, however, that these narratives were partial and partisan as Ellsworth (1989) explains: "partial in the sense that they are unfinished, imperfect, limited; and partial in the sense that they project the interests of 'one side' over others" (p. 305). From a phenomenological perspective, although the goal is to construct a full interpretive description, there is also the recognition that these descriptions are never identical to the lived experience itself (van Manen, 1990). Clearly, the interviews project the interests of the students over those of the teachers, and I made no attempt to "check" the students' accounts (except for August's) with their teachers. Several of the participants recognized that they spoke from partial positions. For example, when I was questioning one participant about the "popular group," she responded by saying that she wasn't part of the popular group and that I really should check with them, but that she would be pleased to offer her observations (Interview: 11/25/98).

My interest was solely with the life-world of these adolescents, their interpretations of their world and the language they used to describe their world. I use the justification provided by Alder and Moulton (1998) for this decision: an interpretive design is used when "research takes place in natural settings and researchers want to know about meaning-making and the points of views of particular people in particular settings" (p. 17). This research was about the points of view of the girls as they negotiated the difficult terrain of adolescence at school.

During the interviews, I followed van Manen's advice for collecting accounts of personal experience by asking the participants to think of specific instances, situations, or events related to the experience of resistance to schooling. Also utilized was Seidman's (1998) model of in-depth phenomenological interviewing. As noted by Seidman (1998), people's behavior becomes meaningful when it is placed in the context of their lives and the lives of those around them. Seidman, then, recommends a three-interview structure for each participant. In the first interview, the context of the participant's experience is established. In initial interviews, I asked the girls to talk about their schooling history by describing some of their experiences related to academic achievement. For example, I asked questions such as, "What do you remember most about elementary school?" and "How did you experience the move from elementary school to junior high?" In the second interview, participants reconstruct the details of their experience within the current context (Seidman, 1998). During the third interview participants reflect on the meaning of their experience (Seidman, 1998).

I did not ask predetermined questions that may have limited the field of inquiry (Fontana & Frey, 1994). Initially, I used prompts to stay oriented to the phenomenon of resistance to schooling. I asked the girls to talk about the kinds of behavior commonly associated with resistance to schooling, such as skipping school and not handing in homework. Very quickly, these interviews became less about resistance to schooling and more about disengagement from school owing to conditions that I had not begun to imagine, such as the complex web of social relationships and effects these conditions produced among the participants. The research became an interviewee-guided investigation of the lived experiences of schooling for the participants (Reinharz, 1992) as I followed the interpretive quality of the interviews: as van Manen (1990) says, certain openness is required in research that allows for choosing directions and exploring techniques, procedures and sources that are not always foreseeable at the outset. New topics and directions emerged from the interviews that begged to be explored. When the participants at both sites repeatedly expressed dissatisfaction with their bodies, I asked them to complete a body image survey. The general themes arising from the survey were taken up in subsequent interviews. In these ways I led the interviewees towards certain themes in their life-world (Kvale, 1983), but these themes had been expressed initially by the participants. The girls had the opportunity to read and discuss their interview transcripts, and often these discussions resulted in additional themes and understandings that were taken up in subsequent interviews.

In addition to individual interviewing, I conducted three focus groups at the Creekwood site in June 1998. Five of the six participants attended these lunch hour discussions (one of the participants had stopped attending school). The purpose of the focus group was two-fold. In the individual interviews, the students had spoken at length of the social organization at school. Clearly, the topic was important for them, and in the first focus group I asked participants to construct a web of the social hierarchy in the school. The participants had previously claimed membership to particular social groups, and I was interested in seeing if their definition and categorization of these groups remained stable as they constructed meaning within the social interaction of the focus group.

Secondly, I was concerned that during the individual interviews, I was providing a sanctioned form of skipping class—that is, the girls were willing to be interviewed as it afforded them opportunities to not attend classes without invoking any of the usual penalties. I found that the girls agreed to sacrifice their free time during lunch hour in order to attend the focus group. Originally I had intended to conduct only one focus group, but the girls were eager to continue these group conversations.

Field Work

Interpretive theory views schools as places where meaning is constructed through the social interaction of people (Bennett & LeCompte, 1990). I viewed the field work as a necessary component to the research, as it allowed me the opportunity to become involved in the participants' daily lives at school and to document their actions within a social context.

My original intent was to document the different forms and styles of resistance that were not accessible through interviewing. I observed and documented the kinds of resistance that are not articulated, those that occur through gesture, action and even silence. But as the focus of the interviews changed, a similar change occurred in the field work. In addition to recording what the girls said about topics that were important to them, I also documented their behavior with respect to these topics. For example, when they spoke about the hierarchy of the social groups in the school, I was then able to attend to the practices of inclusion and exclusion that occurred in the classrooms and the hallways.

Document Analysis

I collected both primary documents (those produced by the participants) and secondary documents (those produced outside the immediate situation by others). Primary documents produced by the participants included samples of school work and notes written to each other and to me. Secondary documents, comprising the Cumulative Files and Confidential Records of the participants, were read as texts that documented the official version of the participants' schooling experiences. Participants' report cards were also collected as secondary documents produced by the participants' teachers. Teachers' comments on these official reports represented the ways in which teachers assigned meaning to the students' lives, illuminating another layer of meaning produced in the social context of the school.

Summary

Taken together, these research activities (interviewing, focus groups, field work, and document collection) at two school sites and involving 10 participants provided multiple meanings about the experience of schooling for adolescent girls. As a participant-observer I was able to conceptualize the behavior of the participants as an expression of social contexts (Reinharz, 1992). As an interviewer, I was able to make their voices audible, and I could explore what I had observed of their actions. Above all, I was able to begin to understand the experiences of the girls from their own points of view (Reinharz, 1992).

Selves in the Field

The field revealed itself to me through the research activities, yet "fieldwork reports will combine a full discussion of what the researcher became in the field with how the field revealed itself to the researcher" (Reinharz, 1997, p. 4). Reinharz criticizes the methodological literature that focuses on the research role in the field while ignoring the variety of attributes that researchers bring to the field: she argues that brought and created selves "shape or obstruct the relationships that the researcher can form and hence the knowledge that can be obtained. Thus, these selves affect the researcher's ability to conduct research" (1997, p. 4). What the researcher brings to the field and becomes in the field is a necessary component to the more complete telling of the research.

Reinharz (1997) identifies three general categories of selves that can be applied to any field setting: research-based selves, brought selves, and situationally created selves: "I propose that we both bring the self to the field and create the self in the field. The self we create in the field is a product of the norms of the social setting and the ways in which the 'research subjects' interact with the selves the researcher brings to the field" (p. 3). I applied Reinharz's categories of selves to both of the research sites in order to frame the ethical problems, questions and dilemmas that are integral parts of the research experience (Lofland & Lofland, 1995) and to explore the tensions that arose between these selves in the field. According to Reinharz (1997):

> Documentation of these processes is essential in fieldwork and does not constitute an unwarranted, narcissistic display. Quite the contrary: Understanding the self in fieldwork releases us from the epistemological tension between unreflexive positivism, on the one hand, and navel gazing, on the other. It will help us document how and why the self is the key fieldwork tool. (p. 18)

Brought Selves

Brought selves include background features of identity that the researcher brings to the field setting (Reinharz, 1997). There are a multitude of potential brought selves in the field: the brought selves discussed in the documentation of the research are those selves that become highlighted in the field. In her research, Reinharz (1997) included gender, age, citizenship, ethnic origin, occupation, and family roles within the category of brought selves, as these were attributes that contributed to her understanding of kibbutz life. The brought selves that became highlighted during my time in the field were being a teacher, being a mother, and being a feminist.

Research-based Selves

Research-based selves are those selves made possible by the nature of the research and the research activities. Being a good listener is an example of a research-based self that emerges from the technique of interviewing (Reinharz, 1997). These are the selves (or roles) typically focused on in the methodological literature. Detailed instructions may be given for being an interviewer, being a participant-observer, or being a document collector (e.g. Lofland & Lofland, 1995). Absent from these accounts is any kind of detailed description of particular dilemmas or problems the researcher may encounter. In response to the often-raised question of what participants should get in return for their cooperation, Lofland and Lofland (1995) reply that "the most common answer has been mundane assistance of one sort or another" (p. 59). I did not find this advice to be particularly helpful when confronted with requests for assistance from participants and their parents that were not, in their eyes, "mundane." The various selves in the field offered a number of possible responses to such requests. As a mother (a brought self), I found it difficult to ignore requests for help by other mothers, even though the inner voices of my research-based selves cautioned against involvement.

Situationally Created Selves

Situationally created selves arise in the field and are created through the interactions of the people (including the researcher) in a particular field setting. Reinharz (1997) describes the situationally created selves that emerged in her fieldwork as being a friend, a psychologist/social worker and a temporary member in the kibbutz where she conducted her research. The situationally created selves that arose in my fieldwork included being an advocate for the participants, a counsellor for participants and their parents, and a caring adult in the community.

I found that I became an advocate for the participants. This was a self created by a number of situations. Adler and Adler (1997) believe that when researchers "encounter behavior committed by others that could be harmful to children, they should step out of the neutral position and attempt to help" (p. 39). I encountered a number of situations at the school that I felt were emotionally and socially harmful to the participants, and on these occasions I attempted to provide assistance when the participants specifically requested my help. The most common request was for me to talk to other teachers because "they just didn't understand."

Tensions

A wide range of selves were thus brought to the field and created in the field. Although Reinharz (1997) states that "the researcher does not know in advance what attributes will be meaningful in the field" (p. 18), I was somewhat prepared for the meaningfulness of a number of brought and research-based selves. I had anticipated that being a feminist, a brought self, would shape my decisions about whether to explore or ignore some of the topics that emerged during the field work. For example, I chose to pursue the issue of body image dissatisfaction instead of focusing on academic issues. I was also prepared to be an attentive listener, a research-based self, a key component of the interviewing process. I was unprepared, however, for the range of situationally created selves that emerged and the ways in which these selves conflicted with brought and research-based selves.

The brought self of teacher became particularly problematic at the Creekwood site, conflicting with self as an advocate of the participants and self as a researcher. As a teacher, I was viewed as a member of the institution by the school staff at Creekwood, and it was difficult to resist what Adler and Adler (1997) call the pressure from institutional gatekeepers to enforce school disciplinary norms. During the research activities, I did not feel it necessary to enforce school rules, particularly when I agreed with the participants that some of the rules, such as no gum-chewing and banning back-packs, were ill-conceived.

Another situationally created self that arose was the perception by some of the school staff that I was a behavioral expert regarding the participants. Many times I was stopped in the hallways by teachers who wanted strategies to use with the girls. I found that being an "expert" was problematic, in that what the teachers were really requesting were ways to make the girls more compliant to their demands (e.g., "How can I make her participate in gym?"). Controlling the girls' behavior was not part of my research agenda, as I was more interested in trying to understand their behavior. When the teachers wanted answers and I responded with questions ("Why do you think she doesn't want to participate?"), the experience was mutually frustrating.

Another tension that emerged in the field arose between being a feminist and being a researcher. Many times in the interviews, the girls uttered "facts" about their world that showed how completely they had internalized cultural myths about gender. They viewed gender as a natural category rather than as a social construction, and unquestioningly attributed certain behaviors to the biological body. According to the participants, "boys are always horny" (Interview: 11/25/98), "boys love girls with big chests. The bigger the better" (Interview: 05/22/98), and "girls are meaner than boys. Boys are more relaxed" (Interview: 06/04/98). I felt that I had to address these kinds of statements, but asking questions was largely unproductive. For example, when I asked about female desire, the participant would not respond and continued to talk about boys' horniness. In the interests of continuing the conversation (the response of a research-based self), I chose to abandon this line of questioning. But my feminist self was left with a sense of unease that I had somehow failed to adequately respond to the ways in which the girls were taking for granted and perpetuating certain sexual stereotypes.

In the closeness/distance debate in the methodological literature, many feminist researchers take the position that closeness with the participants is necessary in order to understand them (Reinharz, 1992). Closeness with the participants, though, can lead to tensions between research-based selves and situationally created selves. As the researcher enters the personal lives of the participants, there occurs a "blurring of the distinction between formal and personal relations" (Reinharz, 1992, p. 263). Correspondingly, I found a blurring between the situationally created self of caring adult and the brought self of researcher. As I entered the personal lives of the girls as a researcher asking questions about their experiences of schooling, an intimacy was created between me and the girls. For the girls, I represented someone who would listen, in marked contrast to what they perceived as a lack of caring relationships between themselves and their teachers. When I finished the formal interviewing phase of the research and the girls continued to seek me out to tell their stories, I felt obliged to listen as we had spent a good deal of time constructing a context wherein they felt comfortable talking. I stopped recording and transcribing our conversations, however, believing that the intimacy created by the research was no longer part of the research. Rather, I had stepped into personal relations with the girls, perhaps filling a void at school created by the absence of caring relationships with adults. As a caring adult I was uncomfortable treating these relationships as "data," although my research self struggled with the decision to turn off the tape recorder.

The greatest tensions between situationally created selves and brought selves in the field occurred when I had to make moral and ethical decisions. Heeding Ball and Wilson's (1996) advice to strive to act in students' best interests presented a moral dilemma. What does it mean to act in a student's best interest?

According to Adler and Adler (1997), "scholars of children's behavior must weigh the moral obligation associated with knowing secrets about children's norm and rule violations with the damage to trust that results when researchers inform on their subjects" (p. 40). Adler and Adler abandoned their research-based selves when they felt that the welfare or moral development of their participants was in jeopardy, and at these times they intervened. At the same time, they acquiesced to remaining silent about children's bullying, exclusion and lying, believing these behaviors to be what they termed "normal" deviance (Adler & Adler, 1997, p. 40). Generally, I followed a similar policy in the field, intervening when I was concerned for a student's welfare and not reporting to school officials behaviors that would fall under the realm of "normal" deviance as described by Adler and Adler. I did not, for example, report instances of students skipping classes on a casual basis, but I did intervene when I became aware that one of the participants had not been attending school for days at a time without her parents' knowledge.

Such decisions about intervention were not without their moral dilemmas, and in these cases I found that brought and created selves were in conflict. As a researcher, I wanted to maintain relationships of trust with my participants. I was careful to protect the identity of participants when I attempted interventions—I did not want to be an "informer." In another case, as a teacher, as a mother, and as a concerned adult in the community, I believed that the use of illegal drugs by one of the participants, a twelve-year-old child, jeopardized her welfare. Clearly, this was a case where intervention was appropriate. But, as Adler and Adler (1997) point out, "children also fall under the moral guidance of their parents" (p. 39), and in this instance the mother permitted her daughter's drug use, reasoning that she would prefer to know where her child was and what she was doing over not having her daughter come home at night. The moral obligation I felt toward this participant conflicted with her mother's sense of moral obligation. I suggested to the mother that she might consider involving an outside agency to assist her in regaining a sense of parental authority. The mother did not believe that this solution would benefit her daughter. I then suggested professional counselling, but this suggestion was not taken up. At that point, I felt that I had exhausted any avenues for intervention. The mother's sense of moral guidance took precedence over my own.

Reinharz (1992) believes that when feminist researchers carefully describe what occurs during research, they will likely discover additional methodological and ethical dilemmas. Using the notion of brought and created selves in the field as a frame to describe the methodological and ethical dilemmas that I encountered allowed me to move beyond traditional discussion of dilemmas that center primarily around the roles of participant-observer and interviewer and to provide a more complete telling. The next step of the complete telling is to provide an account of how collected data were analyzed.

Analysis

The data were analyzed using two approaches. In the first analytical approach, I use relevant anecdotes from interviews and field work to show how the experience of resistance as presented by traditional social science is ill understood by traditional social science. This portion of the analysis can be found in chapter 3.

The second analytical approach involved rewriting the interviews into reconstructed life stories (van Manen, 1990). Each participant's set of transcripts was read and reread in order to uncover the significant events in the student's experience. Asking the question, "What statement(s) or phrase(s) seem particularly essential or revealing about the phenomenon being described?" (van Manen, 1990, p. 93), statements from each transcript were highlighted, blocked by theme and then used to write reconstructed life stories (van Manen, 1990) for each participant. Because of the sheer amount of data generated, these reconstructed life stories were almost as unwieldy as the original transcripts. I further narrowed each participant's reconstructed life story to illustrate only one or two themes from the multitude of themes that were generated. Reading the reconstructed life stories as a set of narratives reveals what I believe to be the key themes generated by the data.

Included in these narratives are cultural artifacts related to the highlighted themes. These artifacts include teachers' comments from report cards, student work samples, and notes written by the students. These narratives became the accounts of the students' experiences of negotiating the difficult terrain of adolescence. In chapters 3 and 4, the individual stories of the participants, who they are and how they see their world, are linked to the ways their interpretations of their world are socially constructed within their schools and their communities. Their stories are also linked to relevant literature in the field.

three
Interpreting Resistance

● ●

To BEGIN THIS CHAPTER, PARTICIPANTS DESCRIBE THEIR EXPERI-
ences of skipping school: I call these "Anecdotes of Truancy." The
anecdotes are then used to show how traditional views of resistance
fail to account for the experiences of the girls in this study. Other
possibilities for resistance are described, along with more recent approaches to theorizing resistance. Finally, a poststructuralist conception of resistance is introduced as an alternative framework from
which to analyze resistance.

Anecdotes of Truancy

Dear Ms. Olafson,

I have done some deep thinking about what situation would work for me
as far as school goes. I think the best situation would not be to switch
schools. I don't think that transferring would work—it would probably
be the same kind of working environment. So I think it would be in my
best interest to go to correspondence. Then I can work at my own pace.
I am hoping to receive all my work for the rest of year and what I need
for grade eight. I really do want to graduate and get a job as a lawyer, but

I honestly can't work happily in this present situation. It's not the work that's the problem, I actually like the work. But I can't cope in this environment. The time you've spent on this with me is much appreciated and very helpful. Thanks for everything.
—Alicia

When I received this fax, Alicia had missed over 40 days of school. The act of skipping school, as presented in the literature from critical theorist and neo-Marxist perspectives, is thought to have a single meaning: it is a "classic" resistant behavior that students employ to avoid their schoolwork and to win physical space from the oppressive conditions of the institution (Contenta, 1993; Everhart, 1983; Sefa Dei et al., 1997; Sun, 1995; Willis, 1977). This interpretation of truancy, however, does not fit with Alicia's experience. In fact, as the following anecdotes demonstrate, the participants' narratives show a multiplicity of meanings attached to their acts of truancy.

*   *   *   *

I miss a lot of school but it's not because I want to. I miss school when I'm needed at home. I try to help out as much as I can, especially now that my dad's been laid off. Last year, Mom was sick and she called the school and they came and told me. I ran to my locker and grabbed everything and I ran out. I just ran out. If my mom needs me I'll come running home. (Lynn)

*   *   *   *

Never once did I skip last year. It never even occurred to me. I would have been way too scared that I would have got caught. But then I got like this huge ego boost and I realized all this power that I had and I thought I could pull it off and I did. Skipping's about the power that I have and now I'm learning how to use it. I didn't even realize that there was power to be had—the school kept it from me. Skipping school is a game to be played. I'm not doing anything wrong except for not being in school. I'm enjoying it. It's fun to get away with things and still pull off the marks. I'm also skipping because I really don't like being here anymore. It's much less complicated to go home than to stay at school. I don't have to deal with anybody. I don't have to be here to solve other people's problems or get myself in trouble with my friends. I'm not involved in any of their little games anymore. In a million ways it's just easier not to go to school. The environment here is really tense. There's a lot of pressures put on everybody and there's a lot of arguments and social things going on. It's just easier to avoid all that. (Angela)

*   *   *   *

We skip Phys. Ed. because it's totally embarrassing. We started skipping the second day of school this year! We don't like people staring. Everybody watches you and makes comments, even the teacher. We can't do all the stuff that everyone else can do and everyone watches. They look because we're slower and they insult us and say mean stuff. Sometimes the teacher makes you go up in front of the class and do a little demo thing. And the whole class comments when you're walking back to your place. When we go to phys. ed. we try to avoid the comments by not doing all the stuff the teacher tells us to do. Because if you don't do the stuff then people can't comment. Sometimes we get our parents to write notes so that we can miss phys. ed. (Diane and Rebecca)

*   *   *   *

As the anecdotes show, the girls in this study skipped school for a myriad of reasons, ranging from the need to help at home to the desire to avoid peers' insults. And as Angela pointed out, it's easier to stay at home than to attend school and deal with the tense environment. In the next section of the chapter, traditional understandings of resistance will be shown to lack explanatory power for the complexities of the anecdotes of truancy.

Undermining Dominant Understandings of Resistance

In the literature, Neo-Marxist and critical theoretical views of resistance have predominated. These traditional conceptions of resistance seek to explain resistance in terms of deep structures such as class and race (Everhart, 1983; Giroux, 1983: McLaren, 2003; Sun, 1995). From the neo-Marxist perspective the dominance of capitalism in the economic sphere is extended in schools: that is, schools are places where students from different social classes learn the skills necessary to occupy their location in the division of labor (Giroux, 1983). From this perspective, students from subordinated positions engage in oppositional behaviors and anti-school tactics in order to win what Willis (1977) calls physical and symbolic space from the institution and the dominant school culture. These oppositional strategies demonstrate symbolic resistance to estranged labor that students experience in much of their daily classroom life (Everhart, 1983). Contenta (1993) describes students with "truant minds" (students who are mentally skipping classes) as learning to cope with the monotonous jobs many of them will take in the future. Giroux (1983, p. 99) explains that neo-Marxist resistance theories attempt to analyze how "determinant socio-economic structures embedded in the dominant society work through the mediations of class and culture in shaping the lived antagonistic experiences of students at the level of everyday life." Thus, working-class "lads" are resistant (Willis, 1977) because they are at odds with the dominant school culture. Students such as these may indeed have the predisposition to resist, maintains Levinson (1998), based on their minority status and their perceptions of labor market opportunities. According to Giroux (1994, p. 38), the dominant school culture is "defined largely through the logic of corporate values and the imperatives of the marketplace." In other words, social relationships in schools replicate the hierarchical division of labor in capitalism: "Schools are destined to legitimate inequality, limit personal development to forms compatible with submission to arbitrary authority, and aid in the process whereby youth are resigned to their fate" (Bowles & Gintis, 1976, p. 266).

Critical perspectives criticize the neo-Marxist view for overemphasizing class. The critical perspective situates resistance in a wider frame that sees structural poverty, racism, and social and cultural differences as significant factors in schooling outcomes (Sefa Dei, Massuca, McIsaac, & Zine, 1997). The oppressive nature of schooling, particularly for minority youth, contributes to student resistance. According to Sefa Dei et al. (1997), Black high school students may become resistant when they experience alienation by virtue of being immersed in predominantly White schools.

Both the critical theorist and neo-Marxist conceptions of resistance can be characterized as structuralist because they seek to explain resistance in terms of deep structures. Collins (1995) describes structuralist conceptions of resistance by noting that "The structuralist conception of resistance sees oppositional behavior as a series of reactions, with oppositional lines clearly drawn, and with teachers and students acting and responding to each other in ways determined by deep structures" (p. 24). From a traditional structuralist perspective, students from subordinated groups collectively and actively resist the dominant school ideology (McLaren, 2003; Sun, 1995). Everhart (1983), Sefa Dei et al. (1997) and Willis (1977) have clearly demonstrated that students from subordinated positions do, in fact, form social groups that attempt to disrupt the dominant school culture. In focusing on what is common to the experience of resistance, these theories operate as simple stories, and, like most simple stories, they leave out a great deal (Nicholson, 1999).

Neither the critical theorist nor neo-Marxist conceptualizations of resistance have recognized the possibility that a single act of resistance, such as skipping school, may have multiple meanings, as the anecdotes of truancy have illustrated. Furthermore, these traditional understandings of resistance fail to account for gender differences in the enactment of resistance and for forms of resistance that are subtle and covert. In other words, common-sense meanings of resistance claimed by critical theorists/Marxists hold that resistance to schooling is enacted in overt and disruptive ways, it is a male phenomenon, and it is almost always the result of subordinate social groups reacting to oppression. These generally accepted representations of resistance have the effect of glossing over rather than revealing a more thoughtful understanding of the nature of the phenomenon (van Manen, 1990).

Resistance as Overt Behavior

In the past, resistance has been typically classified and categorized by the appearance of certain behaviors. For example, "Skipping school, cutting classes, making fun of their teachers, or goofing off in class" are instances of students engaging in resistant behavior at school (Sun, 1995, p. 843). Other "oppositional behaviors" and "anti-school tactics" include arguing with teachers, acting out, truancy, and even violence (Sefa Dei et al., 1997). Much of the previous research has focused on these overt, and often public, behaviors at school as indicators of resistance. Yet very rarely did the girls in this study engage in public forms of resistance. On only one occasion, I witnessed a participant, Sheresa, display her displeasure over an assignment by jumping onto a table, shouting and stomping her feet (Field notes: 03/11/98). The same participant described an incident that led to her suspension from school: "This girl was saying stuff to my friends, so me, my friend, and my other friend, all jumped her. We didn't exactly beat her up. She was fine but then she got us suspended" (Interview: 06/08/98). With the exception of Sheresa, the girls in this study rarely acted out in loud, disruptive, or violent ways at school.

Alpert's (1991) study of resistance in an upper middle-class high school recognizes the appearance of less overt forms of resistance to schooling. Alpert's study describes situations where resistant behaviors appear even though the social-cultural norms of the students' home and school are compatible. Referring to Willis and Giroux, Alpert argues that "explanations of Marxist resistant theories are not appropriate here" (1991, p. 363). Middle-class students also participate in resistance, according to Alpert. Maintaining that "research on resistance seems to ignore less overt resistant phenomena that appear routinely in the daily lives of students and teachers" (1991, p. 350), Alpert describes limited participation in classroom discussions and frequent arguments with teachers as examples of non-revolutionary or subtle forms of resistance in middle-class students. Middle-class resistance is characterized by students who follow "most of the teacher's instructions required for academic success (doing homework, passing tests) while resisting those instructions and procedures that do not endanger academic achievements" (1991, p. 362). Although Alpert identifies subtle forms of resistance and recognizes that resistance occurs outside of working-class students, his theory is "not appropriate here" for describing resistance for the girls in this study. In some cases, the participants seriously jeopardized their success in school by their quiet and unyielding refusal to complete classroom assignments. In these ways, competent readers and writers of middle class status could receive failing grades in language arts.

Resistance as a Male Phenomenon

Previous studies on resistance have focused on boys (Willis, 1977) or have made the assumption that the experience of resistance is identical for both boys and girls. For example, Sun's (1995) Student Resistance to Schooling Inventory consisted of a sample of 236 males and 284 females, but there is no discussion of gender-specific differences in the statistical analysis of the results. Rather, males and females are classified together as "respondents" or "students." The exclusion of women has previously been noted by Giroux (1983):

> Resistance studies generally ignore women and gender to focus primarily on males and class when analyzing domination, struggle, and schooling. This has meant that women are disregarded altogether or that when they are included in such studies it is only in terms that echo the sentiments of the male counter cultural groups being portrayed. (p. 104)

More recently, arguments have been made for including gender in resistance studies. Sefa Dei et al. (1997) note that social positions including race, class, and gender contribute to the multiple identities that students bring to their schooling experiences. These social positions are then subject to multiple forms of oppression which accompany them.

One notable exception to the exclusion of girls in resistance studies is McRobbie's ethnographic study of the dynamics of class and gender in the day-to-day lives of a small group of teenage girls in Birmingham, England, in the late 1970s. The merit of this study, according to McRobbie (1980), is that it had not been done before as previous studies focused on teenage boys. McRobbie (1980) critiqued the male bias of subcultural theorists, such as Willis, noting that although youth culture has been a central strand of cultural studies, the work has remained consistently on male youth cultural forms, and that girls' subcultures have become invisible because the very term "subculture" has acquired strong masculinist overtones (McRobbie & Garber, 1980). McRobbie and Garber concluded that girls have different ways of organizing their cultural lives; they "negotiate a different leisure space and different personal spaces from those inhabited by boys. These in turn offer them different possibilities for 'resistance'" (1980, p. 14). In the next section of the chapter, various possibilities of resistance for girls are described.

Possibilities for Resistance

A number of possibilities for resistance have been described by various theorists and researchers. One such possibility is called "political resistance" by Taylor, Gilligan and Sullivan (1995). These researchers identify two forms of political resistance. Overt political resistance occurs when girls either speak or act against relationships that feel false or act against conventions that require self-sacrifice or silence. Political resistance includes rejection of racial, ethnic, class, and sexual stereotypes (Taylor et al., 1995, p. 26). Covert political resistance occurs when girls outwardly appear to comply with the conventions but do so as a conscious strategy of self-protection (Taylor et al., 1995, p. 26).

In a study of the literacies of junior high girls, Finders (1997) found that note-passing and writing on the rest-room walls served as acts of resistance while also creating strong bonds of solidarity among the girls. Note-passing and graffiti are part of what Finders refers to as the literate underlife of the junior high school, or "those practices that refuse in some way to accept the official view, practices designed and enacted to challenge and disrupt the official expectations" (1997, p. 24). In addition to their participation in the literate underlife, the girls in Finders' study also subtly subverted the officially sanctioned literacies of the school through their disengagement with language arts assignments. Assignments were completed with little regard for the quality of their work, the girls all wanted to know the teacher's minimum expectations, they circulated assignments, they borrowed and bought right answers to avoid "wasting time," and they often loaned or sold essays and short stories to others "in order to work against the institutional sanctions while still maintaining their connection to these sanctions" (Finders, 1997, p. 73). The traditional view of resistance as not doing the work (Willis, 1977) does not fit here because these girls did, in fact, complete their assignments. However, borrowing or buying assignments is equally as subversive as not doing the work, and demonstrates that possibilities for resistance exist in the literate underlife of the classroom.

Another possibility for resistance is silence (Mahoney, 1996): "Silence, then, should not be understood unidimensionally as the condition of disempowerment, or 'being silenced,' but carries the potential for strength and resistance" (p. 624). Students who do not participate in class activities and discussions and "shut down" without being disruptive may be engaging in a form of resistance. But as

Mahoney points out, there is danger to ascribing a single meaning to a girl's silence.

Other covert possibilities for resistance are identified by Finders (1997). In the two groups of girls she studied, Finders found for the most part, the girls embraced the role of the nice, kind and helpful girl while turning to backstage regions to resist. One such backstage region is the literate underlife of the classroom. Resisting intellectual engagement is another form of covert resistance in the backstage region. Finders observed that intellectual rigor, curiosity, or engagement was minimal, and on the rare occasions when a student became intrigued with a language arts project or assignment, she attempted to conceal it. One of her participants "worked very hard to conceal the fact that she was a reader and worked equally hard to construct an image of herself as an uninterested learner" (Finders, p. 72). For adolescent girls, non-participation, borrowing or buying assignments, and concealing intellectual engagement are some of the covert possibilities for avoiding school work. One of the participants in this study outlined three ways to approach class work: public resistance (fighting with the teacher), private resistance (quietly not doing the work), or simply putting up with it:

> Even if I don't like being there I just do the work anyways, I just keep quiet and put up with it. I don't cause any trouble but some kids do if they don't want to do the work. They fight with the teachers over the work. So you can either shut up and do the work, put up a fight or just sit there and do nothing. (Emma: 06/15/98)

As Emma points out, the possibilities for resistance are not limited to overt acts. Rather, girls may engage in forms of resistance that are more subtle than those described in earlier studies focusing on boys.

Resistance as Socially Constructed and Agentic

In contrast to structuralist perspectives, the poststructuralist view of resistance recognizes that resistance is socially constructed and agentic (Collins, 1995). Collins argues that we must drop the deep-structure-variety of political resistance and study resistance as it is being constituted in elementary and middle schools. Ferrell (1995) agrees, insisting that instances of resistance must be located in the particular activities and meanings of daily life and be fixed with particular cultural and political contexts. Resistance from this view recognizes that "resistant students are not resistant all by themselves. Resistance is constituted through discourse, and peers and teachers collaborate in its construction" (Collins, p. 25). Resistance can be constituted within the teacher-student relationship, for example. A teacher's response to a student's resistant behavior may influence further acts and can actually increase resistant behavior, as described by Bennett and LeCompte (1990): "Resistance may begin with simple non-conforming behavior, and then be transformed into resistance by the negative responses of school staff" (p. 108). Within the classroom, direct displays of power by a teacher may also contribute to the construction of resistance. Davies (1993) says that in any naming of a direction, its opposite is also opened up as an unstated possibility. In relation to direct displays of power, says Davies, a child can conceive of resistance more readily.

Another way that resistance is constructed in the classroom is through the instructional strategies adopted by the teacher. Not doing the work is a classic sign of resistance; however, the tasks students are asked to do are rarely questioned, nor are students asked for their reasons for not doing the work. A student may resist completing a math worksheet in dividing decimals, for example, because she is already competent in that skill owing to the fact that she has received instruction in dividing decimals for three consecutive years. Alicia, for example, failed to see the purpose in completing fifty division questions from the textbook when she had already mastered the skill (Alicia: 12/02/97). In the face of this kind of logical non-compliance, teachers are at a loss: "Many teachers are unused to reasoned defiance, and a school-aged 'critical thinker' is likely to be viewed with suspicion" (Epp, 1996, p. 10).

In addition to the teacher's instructional strategies and assigned tasks, the amount of school work required may also lead to avoidance. Participants in this study reported feeling overwhelmed when a number of assignments were due at the same time, and responded by "shutting down" (Field notes: 02/26/98). When faced with multiple and competing deadlines, some students were not able to prioritize tasks and consequently ended up with very few tasks reaching completion.

Resistance in the classroom may also arise in response to a classroom climate that does not foster critical thinking. Fine (1991, p. 38), observes that "When test rules and correct answers are privileged over student beliefs and opinions, when sarcasm reigns as pedagogy, students may resist through 'insubordination'…or through vacant stares."

In these examples of resistance being constructed in the classroom, it is primarily the nature of the teacher-student interactions that "cause" resistance. Clearly, an asymmetrical teacher-student relationship leads to spiraling power struggles:

> Most of the teachers keep bugging me to get my work done. You have to do it their way, a certain way, and if you don't then you're just going to get punished for it. And it has to be done by a certain time. It just turns me off. Sometimes, I refuse to do the work. When they challenge me, I feel like I have to challenge them right back. It's my life, it's my school work. It just bugs me how they think they have control over our lives. (Raye: 11/04/97)

In this example, Raye articulates the relationship between the teacher's expectations for work and the ways in which she responds to this relationship. In the face of what Raye perceives to be unreasonable demands (i.e., one "right" way, one deadline) and the teacher's unwillingness to negotiate, Raye notes that she sometimes chooses to refuse to complete the assignment.

But, once again, focusing on a unifying theme (the social construction of resistance through the teacher-student relationship) serves to conceal other relationships in the classroom through which resistance might be constructed, such as those that occur between students. One of the girls in the study resisted oral presentations because of the nature of her relationships with her classmates:

> I refuse to do oral presentations. You just worry that you're going to sound really stupid in front of the whole class. If you're stressed out you can't do as good a job because you're worried about what the other kids are going to think. And when you don't do a good job, then they'll tease you and make comments and put you down and stuff. So if I have a presentation in Language Arts I skip the whole afternoon because if I just skipped Language Arts and then went back, I'd get caught (Interview: 12/10/98).

Resistance, then, may also be constructed in the social relationships between students.

The poststructuralist view that resistance is agentic is another claim that reveals and conceals particularities of the experience of resistance. Human agency, says Collins (1995), is "found in particular events, culturally constituted yet situationally improvised choices of particular persons" (p. 4). In schools, however, students are often deprived of their agency. Because they are framed as students, "their subject status is never fully guaranteed. It is always partial and conditional. They can be positioned as beings without agency and autonomy at any moment, usually when they are read by adults as not knowing how they should behave" (Davies, 1993, p. 9). Acts of resistance, interpreted from a poststructuralist perspective, can be read as instances where students attempt to act with agency. Fine (1991), for example, believes that the act of dropping out could be recast as a strategy for students taking control of lives fundamentally out of control. The students in Sefa Dei et al.'s study (1997) described skipping class, arguing with teachers, and even dropping out as occasions where they were able to most significantly tap into their reserves of self-confidence and self-esteem. Sun (1995) supports the agency argument, noting that resistance to school is the only way to gain autonomy in an oppressive environment.

However, individual decisions to engage in resistant behavior may not always be the attempt to gain autonomy. Rather, some students' actions may leave them feeling less confident. In a telephone conversation with one of the girls in the current study, I was not left with the sense that Diane had taken control of her life by dropping out of school. She did not seem to view her decision as a personal choice: the conditions at the school, her relationships with her peers, and the perceived lack of caring by her teachers were all factors that contributed to the decision to leave school. Diane did not drop out of school; she was "pushed out of school all together by an unresponsive institution" (Bennett & LeCompte, 1990, p. 110). Interpreting dropping out of school solely as an act of agency conceals the role that the institution may play in this process.

Recent Theorizing

More recent approaches to theorizing resistance include a psychoanalytic notion of resistance (Ellsworth, 1997; Pitt, 1998), a sociolinguistic perspective (Rampton, 1996), a pragmatist revisioning of resistance theory (Abowitz, 2000), and a moral conception of resistance (Olafson & Field, 2003).

From the psychoanalytic perspective, Pitt (1998) studied women's engagement in academic feminist knowledge. As a result of her work, she defined resistance as the process of managing psychic conflict. Similarly, Ellsworth (1997) has argued that the individual psyche plays a role in resistance. She criticizes sociologists of education for not thinking of resistance "in terms of what happens in the space of difference between the outside (the social) and the inside (the individual psyche)" (Ellsworth, 1997, p. 47). In interpreting resistance, the "inside" is largely ignored; certainly, poststructuralist perspectives emphasize the "outside," or the ways in which resistance is socially constructed. The desire to ignore (Felman, 1987), for example, may be an instance of resistance to learning based on unconscious forces. Here, ignorance is "linked to what is not remembered, what will not be memorized. But what will not be memorized is tied up with repression, with the imperative to forget—the imperative to exclude from consciousness, not admit to knowledge" (Felman, 1987, p. 79).

The unconscious may speak in another way. According to Gilligan (1991), girls often use the phrase "I don't know" to cover knowledge that they believe may be dangerous. What kind of knowledge might be dangerous in the lives of adolescent girls? Retrospectively, a striking feature in my conversations with the participants was the almost complete lack of discussion of sexuality. Taylor et al. (1995) note that it is unusual for girls to ask questions and to speak openly about what they are thinking and feeling in their bodies, and that "the kinds of questions girls may have are not likely to be answered in health and sex education classes, which for the most part leave out the possibilities of girls' desire" (p. 115). Neither I nor the participants attended to the possibilities of girls' desire. Perhaps this desire to ignore was part of our mutual repression and unconscious forces of which we were not aware. At any rate, I acknowledge that my focus on the words and actions of the participants—on that which was directly observable to me—is a limitation of this study. At the same time, though, I also acknowledge the possibility that much of the participants' thought and behavior is based on unconscious forces.

From a sociolinguistic perspective, Rampton (1996) studied British-born male adolescents of Indian and Pakistani descent. He found that these boys put on strong Indian accents when talking to White adults in order to disturb smooth discursive interactions. Rampton highlights the playful nature of such resistance and the ways in which it is constructed discursively. Here, Rampton shows how sociolinguistic discourse analysis can provide a useful set of tools for studying resistance.

Abowitz (2000) uses Dewey's theories of inquiry and communication to reinterpret resistance. She notes that a transactional view of resistance recognizes multiple and shifting identities and that "resistant acts take on complex and often contradictory meanings for those who experience them, including those authorities who react in official and unofficial ways to these acts" (p. 902). Interpreting resistance from this framework, notes Abowitz, can promote school-based inquiry of resistance that moves beyond simple avoidance or punishment. School-based inquiry into the phenomenon is certainly one that will move the field beyond some of the more traditional conceptions of resistance.

Another example of reinterpreting resistance comes from Olafson and Field (2003). They found that school personnel relied on the institution's moral code (the application and enforcement of rules and regulations) when responding to instances of resistance without taking into account circumstances surrounding resistance. In a moral revisioning of resistance, Olafson and Field argue that student resistance to schooling must be situated within an ethical framework, so that the practice of being attuned to particular concrete conditions and relationships, and making sensitive, informed choices about what is right and good becomes a moral imperative in schools.

Multiple Meanings

What these newer perspectives demonstrate is that resistance theorizing continues to occur in part because previous theories lack explanatory power. As Abowitz (2000) notes, "the interruption of old meanings signal that new meanings are in the making" (p. 899). As the anecdotes of truancy revealed, skipping school is not necessarily in response to the rule of the institution as critical theorists and neo-Marxists have traditionally asserted. Angela's belief that skipping school is a game of power is the account most closely aligned with the critical theorist's interpretation of skipping. Her growing recognition that she is not powerless in the face of the institution and that she can "subvert dominant norms" (Sefa Dei et al., 1997, p. 25) can be read as "an attempt to wrestle some control from a system that determines where students should be, when they should be there, and what they should do while they're there" (Contenta, 1993, p. 43). At this layer of meaning, Angela's acts of skipping are intended to subvert institutional authority.

Yet Angela's story also points to another layer of meaning, similar to that stated by Alicia, that missing school is a means to avoid the social pressures of schooling. Neither Angela nor Alicia skipped school to avoid completing school assignments. They were not generally rejecting their school work, in contrast to Willis' (1977) interpretation of truancy. They continued to be concerned about their academic progress and to ensure that they complete their school work. Contenta (1993) maintains that "as a general rule, the kids who reject the rules at any school are made up of those who are not in what the school hierarchy and society consider a winning stream of study" (p. 42). Angela and Alicia, straight "A" students in grade seven, would surely disagree that they are in a "losing" stream of study.

Rebecca and Diane, on the other hand, skipped particular classes in order to avoid participation in physical education. Traditional conceptions might assume their resistance to physical education is a way to express their entrenched general and personal opposition to authority (Willis, 1977). Their opposition, however, is directed primarily at their peers and not at their teacher. Avoidance of the "work" of physical education did not challenge dominant institutional norms and practices as Sefa Dei et al. (1997) believe but challenged instead the practices of their peers. Much resistance is aimless (Contenta, 1993; Willis, 1977), but Rebecca and Diane employed deliberate strategies such as bringing notes from home, avoiding participation in class, and not attending physical education classes, to ensure that they would not be faced with their classmates' ridicule.

Summary

Dominant meanings of resistance presented by critical theorist/ Marxist and poststructuralist theories should not be completely discounted. The literature and my own research clearly document that these meanings occur at the level of the classroom with great regularity. What is dangerous, though, is that these theories are presented as unitary discourses, thereby concealing what Nicholson (1999) calls the identification of multiple meanings in the present. My intention is to make "spaces for exceptions found in the experiences and classrooms of teachers and students" (Gore, 1993, p. 49), allowing some of these multiple meanings to be revealed. Insights from Foucault's concept of resistance are used in order to restore resistance to its original complexity.*

Using Foucauldian insights permits exploring the relationship between power and resistance; that is, the notion that resistance is intimately connected to the play of power. In fact, resistance is in the same place as power, and there are no relations of power without resistance (Foucault, 1980). Within the vast network of power relationships in the school (the different forms and levels of power that will be described in chapter 5), multiple forms of resistance are possible. Resistance does not have univocal nature: rather, forms of resistance emerge against different forms of power (Foucault, 1982a).

Resistance as the compatriot of power (Foucault, 1980), though, is not the same as resistance being "the other side of power" as Haber (1996, p. 153) insists. Power and resistance are not in a disembodied duel, according to Gupta and Ferguson (1997). They find it useful to think of resistance as an "experience that constructs and reconstructs the identity of subjects" (1997, p. 18). The idea that resistance can be constitutive of identity (as the refusal of particular forms of

---

* Foucault's conception of resistance is not without its difficulties. Critics have claimed, for example, that he "provided no convincing account of how resistance to power is possible" (Sawicki, 1996, p. 162). In response to this criticism, I argue that Foucault maintained that well-timed local actions were most effective and that each struggle develops around a particular source of power: "to speak on this subject, to force the institutionalized networks to listen, to produce names, to point the finger of accusation, to find targets, is the first step in the reversal of power and the initiation of new struggles against existing forms of power" (1977, p. 214). The strength of Foucault's work lies not in providing a step-by-step account of how an individual might engage in a struggle against a form of power but in providing the conceptual tools by which we might begin to identify forms of power and the struggles engaged in by particular individuals.

subjectivity) will be revisited in chapter 6. Conceptualizing resistance as experience allows for a more complex interpretation of resistance, one that is not completely focused on whether or not it is a good thing or a bad thing (Lindquist, 1994) or on defining exactly what it is and what it is not (Giroux, 1983).

As the anecdotes of truancy revealed, there are multiple meanings attached to the experience of skipping school. In some cases, truancy emerged as a response against a form of institutional power. At other times ("I can't cope in this environment"), the particular form of power being struggled against is the exercise of power within the peer group. In these instances, the social pressures of schooling are being resisted. It is Foucault's conceptualization of resistance that allows multiple interpretations. This notion of resistance will be revisited in chapter 5, where its connection to forms of power is discussed as a part of the theoretical framework. In the next chapter, the process of thematic analysis as the next phase of analysis is described.

four

Reconstructing Life Stories

● ●

Introduction

SLENDERNESS, PERFECTION, POPULARITY, ACCEPTANCE, RELATION-
ships with others: these were the themes that emerged repeatedly
during my conversations with the girls in this study. They were
clearly topics of significance to the participants, and they emerged
as common patterns between participants and school sites. The following excerpts from the data highlight these themes.

Focus Group Transcript

May 22, 1998

Participant: You can get a perfect body by going into surgery, but by
yourself, from just eating right and exercising, you can't get it. But if you
go into surgery, you can have anything you want.
Participant: Thanks to modern-day technology we have the power.
Participant: You can stay skinny but you can't be ideal. You can't change
the size of your hips and chest and stuff without surgery.
Lori: Does anyone have a perfect body?

Participant: No one, there's not a single person. Everybody has at least one weird feature wrong with them. Like my feet. They're just weird. My toes are too long.

Participant: I'd change my ears. My ears aren't so bad anymore but when I was littler they were like the same size.

Participant: I'd change my belly flub. I have this belly flub thing.

Participant: I'd be 100% thinner. Everything about me would be thinner. I even have a fat forehead. Everything about me is fat. So I'd just be thinner.

Participant: I'd change my nose. I don't like my nose. It's big.

Participant: I wish my teeth were straight without having to do anything about it.

Participant: There's nothing I like about my body. Nothing. Not even my eye color.

*   *   *   *

Interview Transcript (Brenda)

November 25, 1998

Being popular means being accepted. Part of being popular is being attractive to boys. The popular group is the biggest group at school. They all dress cool. They group together and they exclude other people, like the Pathetic Wannabes. They're the people that follow the popular group around, trying to be like them and get accepted.

*   *   *   *

Telephone Conversation (Diane)

January 21, 1999

I'm never going back to that school. I'm doing home schooling now, but I don't know how I'm going to get all the work done without any help. The teacher knew I'd be upset when they moved my best friend, Rebecca, into a different class: Ms. Green wouldn't even look me in the eye. Now I have no friends in that class. The teachers cared more about Rebecca than me, and Mr. Miller didn't care about anyone.

*   *   *   *

I read and reread each participant's set of transcripts to uncover particular events and statements in relation to these themes. I followed van Manen's (1990) approach to thematic analysis: reflection on the texts produced by the conversational interviews in order to uncover their thematic aspects or the elements that occurred frequently in the texts. First, I used the selective reading approach (van Manen, 1990), reading each girl's set of transcripts several times, asking "What statement(s) or phrase(s) seem particularly essential or revealing about the phenomenon being described?" These statements were highlighted, and each set of transcripts became a text of these highlighted statements. Next, the highlighted transcripts were reworked into what van Manen (1990) calls a reconstructed life story for each of the girls. The format of these narratives follows Seidman's structure for phenomenological interviewing in that the reconstructed life story begins with an account of previous schooling context, moves to current experiences, and then concludes with the participant's discussion of thinking about her future in terms of schooling and career. This analytical approach resulted in a reconstructed life story (van Manen, 1990) for each participant. I was left with ten reconstructed life stories, or narratives, ranging in length from two to ten pages. The reconstructed life stories are an attempt to uncover and describe the structures of lived experience and necessarily included an analysis of what was most common to the experience (van Manen, 1990). They are lived experience descriptions that highlight recurring themes in the interviews. In the next section of the paper, the reconstructed life stories of two of the girls, Angela and Sheresa, are presented (See the Appendix for the reconstructed life stories of the other eight girls). As mentioned previously, the reconstructed life stories follow the general format of beginning with the participant's recollection of significant schooling experiences, followed by a description of the current context of schooling. The reconstructed life stories conclude with the participants' looking forward into the future of their schooling.

Angela and Sheresa

Angela and Sheresa's reconstructed life stories were chosen to present in detail for several reasons. They represent each of the sites:

Angela attended seventh grade at Creekwood while Sheresa was an eighth grade student at Kingwood. Both Angela and Sheresa were "key informants" at their respective sites. In addition to being articulate about their experiences they also demonstrated knowledge about their settings that was corroborated by their peers. They seemed to have a good understanding of the social context at their schools. Angela had not experienced any official difficulties academically or socially at Creekwood. Her acts of resistance occurred primarily underground. On the other hand, Sheresa experienced academic and social problems. She had been expelled from her previous school and began attending Kingwood at mid year. Sheresa's acts of resistance were more overt, ranging from physical fighting to walking out of the classroom. Angela and Sheresa, very different in many respects, discussed many common themes in their interviews.

Angela participated in seven individual interviews and three focus groups at Creekwood. Extensive documents were collected related to her schooling, including her final report card for seventh grade and several written assignments that she consented to have photocopied. Angela was bright and vivacious. She self-identified as being in the popular group, and the other girls at Creekwood acknowledged her popularity. When discussing the social hierarcy at Creekwood during an individual interview with one of the other participants, Raye suggested that I should check with Angela, because "she knows everything that's going on in this school." In seventh grade, Angela had 12.5 recorded absences. Her final grades were primarily A's, except for a B in physical education and a B+ in math. Comments provided on the report card by her teachers were overwhelmingly positive. Four of her teachers included this comment on her report card: "It has been a pleasure working with you this term." Other comments included, "Your great attitude and effort contributed positively to our classroom" and "A confident and independent student."

Sheresa, in the eighth grade at Kingwood, was also a key informant. During five months of observations at the site, I observed that she demonstrated leadership skills within Mr. Kim's classroom. She participated in three individual interviews. I was not able to collect any documents related to Sheresa's schooling experiences. Her cumulative record was unavailable as it had not arrived from her previous school.

Angela's Reconstructed Life Story

Never once did I skip last year. It never even occurred to me. I would have been way too scared that I would have got caught. But then I got like this huge ego boost right, and I realized all this power that I had and I thought I could pull it off and I did. I got busted a few times, but we got out of it. There's a group of kids that skip. The powerful kids. Maybe that's why Miss C. doesn't like me, because I have so much power over her. I have a lot of power here. I control other students, and I can control teachers, and I can control my parents. Through manipulation. It bothers me a lot but if it keeps me out of trouble, I mean, I'm getting what I want here and I'm still getting good marks. I didn't even realize it that there was power to be had.

Skipping school is a game to be played. I hope I don't ruin my reputation by skipping school. I'm walking a pretty fine line. Like I don't want people to think that I'm doing things that I'm not supposed to just because I'm not in school. And I'm worried about stereotypes about children that skip school that I'll be, you know, doing drugs or drinking all day or having beebee gun fights. We're not doing anything wrong except not being in school. And I'm enjoying it and it's fun. It's fun to get away with things. And to still pull off the marks. I've figured out that I can actually hand in assignments even when I'm not here. I've had people pick up things for me in classes, assignments, grab extra sheets for me, and they are more than willing to do it. My friends are covering for me. And when I'm not there, like when I'm skipping, they'll tell the teachers that I'm sick or that I wasn't feeling well or I had a dentist appointment or something.

The whole skipping thing started this year. I think it was the middle of September. It was a project that I really didn't want to do, it was a social project, and we had been working on it, and she just talked forever; she just talked, the same thing over and over again. We had double social first class and it was like, no, I'm not going. I can't do this anymore. It's a waste of my time. I'm going to go work on my project at home, I get a lot more done. And that morning I did. I got almost my project completely finished. I had everything I needed, and she talked all morning from what I hear. She did exactly what we thought she would do. So it had immediate payoff, and I think that was kind of not a good thing. And I didn't get caught. I didn't get caught until the second or third time and we talked our way out of it, and since then, we don't even worry about it. There's no real reason for me to be here. The lessons are boring. And so I don't feel like I have to soak up that extra information that I'm getting from her lecturing. I can get everything from the textbook and still pass with good marks. I'm not just passing either; I'm getting about 80% on everything. Marks are important to me even if I'm not here. Failing my classes is not an option. Because then I can't justify leaving school. If I can get my assignments done and still get good marks, then I don't have a reason to be here, but if I'm not getting good marks, I have to be here to learn these things. I have no excuse.

I'm skipping because I really don't like being here anymore. It's much less complicated to go home than to stay in school. I don't have to deal with anybody. I don't have to, you know, be here to solve other people's problems or get myself into trouble with my friends. You know, I still talk to them and everything but I'm not involved in any of their little games anymore. It's much easier to just avoid all that. In a million ways it's easier just to not go to school. The environment here is really tense. There's a lot of pressure put on everybody. Outside the classroom. There's a lot of arguments and social things going on. The tension isn't actual academic things. There's no pressure on me to do anything academic.

Here at school, for example, girls are obsessive about their appearance. Nobody likes how they look. Even the perfect body doesn't make you happy, but if I were thinner, I'd have it all. When we read YM, we like to emulate the model's makeup. It makes you feel cool. When we see these athletic good-looking people having fun in their ads, we tend to think if our body image is the same as theirs we will have fun and be popular too. But it's not just body image that we try to imitate either. We try to copy clothes and makeup and overall personality. Me personally, I am not affected by the media on a very severe level. I'm fat. I wish that I could say I'm thin enough. I don't like how I look. I know I'm clumsy and not that smart. I accept who I am. That's the reason I feel competent.

I don't like P.E. Everyone's always watching. It makes you really self-conscious. You're always being evaluated by teachers and peers. I like soccer and I like floor hockey. When I don't have to take P.E.

I'm not going to and hope that I can stay fit by myself. You get made fun of in P.E. because you look stupid. I don't like P.E.

I find it very difficult to describe the social patterns at our school. I have decided that it can't be fully understood unless it is experienced. It seems very simple at first, but there are at least a million of the "unwritten" rules of social webbing that make it exceedingly complex. It starts out like this—you hang around with people who have common interests. There are not many of these large groups to choose from. Likely six in grade seven. From there it gets very complicated. A lot of stereotyping and politics comes into play. You may not like the people you end up with, but it is VERY hard to beat this system and change groups How much of an individual you can be depends on what group you are in. I think the more popular you are, the easier it is to be an individual because you're already accepted as what you are—you're cool. Everyone knows that the popular boys are more popular than the popular girls at school because everybody knows that girls live for boys.

Sheresa's Reconstructed Life Story

I've missed three months of school this year. I've only been at this school for about two months and 2 weeks. I was expelled from my old school, like you get suspended three times and then you're automatically expelled. It's part of a zero tolerance policy, three strikes and you're out. I think it bites. It's stupid. Three strikes you're out. The first time I got suspended was when I got back from Turning Points. It's a special program that goes for two months and they like let you work at your own pace and all that other fun stuff, and when I got back from Turning Points, this girl was saying stuff to my friends, so me, my friend, and my other friend, all jumped her. She was in Grade 9. We didn't exactly beat her up. She was fine but then she got us suspended. And then the second time I was suspended is because I didn't work hard enough, and the third time I got suspended is because we had a substitute in math class and he couldn't get the class to be quiet. So I told the class to be quiet and he started yelling at me, "Oh, how would you like to be overruled by a 13 year old, blah, blah, blah." Some guys were throwing glue balls at the teacher in class. They were throwing them, and they didn't even get expelled. I was just telling them to be quiet. I'm the only one that got expelled and there was ten people that went down. And then the Assistant Principal came down and she told me to go to the office and then she asked me where my locker was, so I was standing right there and I'm like why. And she's like, you're getting suspended. And I'm like no, I'm not. I thought I was just helping the sub. And then I threw my books in the garbage, grabbed my stuff, and walked out. And never went back. That third suspension wasn't all that fair.

I'm more concerned about my looks now than when I was in elementary school. Like even though I know that tanning beds increase your chance of cancer I go anyways because I hate being very white. And at school everything is based on your appearance. If a new person comes, you're judged on what you look like. It's hard to be in a place where you're judged on appearance and you can't be yourself. I'm a little more mature, so I dress in my own way.

Another stupid thing is the dress code rules. You're not allowed to show your belly button or your shoulders. And when you wear shorts they have to come down to there. Because teenage boys are going through hormones and they'll think something. That's a crock, that boys can't control their hormones. They can if they wanted to. That's what they say, teenage boys can't be trusted. They say that it would be our fault if something happened. I don't think it would. Because when you wear them outside of school nothing happens.

The whole thing about like the school telling you how to dress and how to act and how to behave, that just makes us worse. Because if you're getting told to do something then the more they tell you not to do something, the more you're going to do it. If the school trusted us, well then they'd get trusted. I don't think it would be chaos because they'll respect the teachers for respecting their thoughts. If teachers respected students, the students would respect teachers. I guess you have to give respect before you get it. A lot of junior high teachers don't understand that.

I can't work in certain environments. Sometimes people will just pick at you and it gets you mad…then I can't work. One day I wanted to go home because I didn't feel like staying at school right, this one guy was bugging me or something, so I threw a book at him. A lot of the boys are always bugging me and it just gets to the point where I lose it. It bothers me and I react. They say stuff like, "skanky whore."

Or they'll mock me. They'll just start picking on me. Or throwing me in puddles when it's raining, getting my clothes drenched. And the girls can be mean too. When I came back to school after getting suspended, five chicks jumped me. They thought I was giving them dirty looks and that I was having problems with them. I had to get stitches on my eyebrow, but I didn't hurt them.

In my other school, they'd never let me have a time out and they never let me go out in the hallway, and that's when I'd get in trouble. Here, when I feel I need a time out, I can take it. So things don't get to the point where I have to be suspended because I can cool down before I start being totally out of control. I worry about my temper when I'm in a grouchy mood. Sometime I go work somewhere else. Depends what kind of mood I'm in. Like when I want to work one day, I'll just go by myself and sit in part of the room, or I have to work in the library. And Mr. Kim lets me do that. And if I don't understand then I always ask Mr. Kim to help me. When we have to have everything done, I get frustrated so Mr. Kim just tells me to bring it in the next day. I do. But sometime I don't bother doing an assignment because it's not worth your time. Like this thing in Humanities. I'm not going to do that. She wants a retelling of a story that she read to us like a week ago and we have to rewrite it. Like I'm going to remember all of that.

I'm not sure about what's going to happen next year. I think that I'm supposed to go back to my other school but I don't want to. I might be going to some other kind of program. I am going to try and make it through high school and then I want to be a kindergarten teacher or a photographer.

*   *   *   *

The contrasts between the two girls are striking. Angela was a high achiever who did not cause any problems for her parents or teachers, while Sheresa had a lengthy history of behavioral problems and low achievement, by her own admission. More striking than the differences though, are the commonalities between the accounts of the two girls. Both questioned some of the institutional aspects of schooling, including school rules and the "work" of school that was perceived as boring or meaningless. Socially, they described the school environment as complicated and tense, whether it was getting picked on or mocked by boys (Sheresa) or arguing and "playing little games" with peers (Angela). One's physical appearance was given great importance by Angela and Sheresa. And both girls described how they wanted to stay at home rather than go to school. Resistance to schooling, then, seemed to be related to the three general themes of institutional aspects of schooling, a socially tense environment, and pressure to conform to expectations of appearance. These structures of lived experience are found in the reconstructed life stories of the other eight participants, and the analysis of what is most common (van Manen, 1990) is provided in the next chapter.

five

Theoretical Framework
Bodies, Relationships of Power, and Regimes of Truth

● ●

Introduction

THROUGH THE GIRLS' RECONSTRUCTED LIFE STORIES, I HAD A better sense of their experiences of schooling, and I came to understand that they attached importance to particular issues around slenderness, perfection, popularity, acceptance and care. But I was not at all sure how these themes might be related to one another and to a larger order. In this chapter, the themes represented in the reconstructed life stories are linked theoretically to a conception of the body and to Foucault's concept of resistance that is tied to relational power and regimes of truth, thus providing a theoretical framework through which to view bodies and subjectivities of adolescent girls.

The focus group on May 22, 1998, at the Creekwood site proved to be a catalyst for making sense of the reams of blocked and themed data. During this focus group, the girls had expressed great unhappiness with their own bodies, thus replicating the findings of many other researchers and theorists (e.g., AAUW Report, 1992; Bordo, 1993; Bordo, 1997; Debold, 1995; Jaffee & Lutter, 1995; Maracek & Arcuri, 1995; Nicholls, 1996; Nichter & Vuckovic, 1994). In addition to expressing deep dissatisfaction with their bodies, the girls also spoke of their willingness to undergo plastic surgery, if they had the resources to do so, in order to bring them closer to achieving the perfect body. All of the girls wished they could change aspects of their bodies that were genetically determined, such as "big bones" (Focus Group: 05/22/98). Overall, they agreed with the sentiments of one participant who sighed, "I wish that I could say that I'm thin enough or pretty enough" (Focus Group: 05/22/98). The beauty myth (Wolf, 1991) appeared to be flourishing at the Creekwood site, much to my disbelief. I introduced these themes of the body at the Kingwood site. These conversations were remarkably similar to those at Creekwood. The participants at both sites were overwhelmingly concerned about the appearance of their bodies, and their body talk compelled me to explore the concept of the body as a means by which I could understand the relationship between the significant events in the lives of these girls. Searching to connect these themes to a larger frame, I used the concept of the body to begin to develop a theoretical framework.

Bodies

I tried to avoid the Western biomedical model that separates body from self and the concept of the unruly body that requires self-control (Sault, 1994). Instead, I used Kirk's (1993) concept that the body is in culture and in nature simultaneously. Kirk explains this concept using examples such as body shape, skin color and racial characteristics (the body in nature), noting that "physical appearance is not only widely utilized as a means of summing up a person's character, but body shapes more generally have over time come to act as symbols, signifying particular social values" (1993, p. 6). Appearance and bodily movements are interpreted according to cultural and social values; in these ways, the body is simultaneously in nature and in culture (Kirk, 1993). In other words, as Bordo (1997) maintains, bodies speak to us: we respond not only to particular body parts or configurations (the body in nature) but also to the meanings they carry for us. These meanings are specific to cultural contexts. One way that people experience and understand bodies is accordance with culturally defined body images and "each different language encodes a set of culturally relative premises about body ideals" (Sault, 1994, p. 12). Many of the participants in this study recognized the concept of the body as simultaneously in culture and in nature. For example, Angela noted that she was fat (the body in nature) and added that "People don't approve of my appearance because of my size" (Interview: 06/16/98).

Neither can the body be understood as separate from the mind. Grosz (1994) maintains that the work of neurologists, psychologists, and psychoanalysts has resulted in a new term, "body image," that mediates the mind/body polarization. According to Grosz (1994), this work demonstrates that body image requires input from both mind and body poles in order to be effective:

> The body image does not map a biological body onto a psychosocial domain, providing a kind of translation of material into conceptual terms; rather, it attests to the necessary interconstituency of each for the other, the radical inseparability of biological from psychical elements, the mutual dependence of the psychical and the biological. (p. 85)

In addition to the mutual dependence of the psychical and the biological, the anthropological perspective on body image adds the notion that body image and social relationships are reciprocally related:

> A person's social relationships and body image are reciprocally related and grow together, with a change in one reflected by a change in the other. The body image is not localized in the mind or the brain but is distributed throughout the whole body, the whole person, and the person's social relationships. The body image system is dynamic, interactive, and so closely integrated that neither body image nor social relations has priority or precedence over the other. (Sault, 1994, p. 18)

The concept of the body used in this study, then, is one that views the body as simultaneously in nature and in culture, following Kirk (1993), and as psychically, biologically and socially interrelated (Grosz, 1994; Sault, 1994). Bodies are the products of these biological, cultural and social interactions.

Constituting Bodies/Constituting Subjects

The body is culturally, socially and historically constituted (Grosz, 1994; Kirk, 1993), thus producing bodies that Grosz calls determinate types. Grosz (1994) describes how bodies are produced as the direct effects of historical, cultural and social factors:

> Bodies cannot be adequately understood as historical, precultural, or natural objects in any simple way; they are not only inscribed, marked, engraved, by social pressures external to them but are the products, the direct effects, of the very social constitution of nature itself. It is not simply that the body is represented in a variety of ways according to historical, social, and cultural exigencies while it remains basically the same; these factors actively produce the body as a body of a determinate type. (p. x)

According to Kirk (1993), the institution of school is central to the process of constructing the body: "It is largely through educational processes, formal and informal, that the normative values surrounding the body are sustained. Schools are important sites in which these processes are worked through and institutionalized" (p. 3). The themes of slenderness, perfection, popularity, acceptance, and relationships with others highlight the cultural, social and institutional interactions that produce bodies of determinate types: bodies that are thin, pretty and popular. Bodily practices surrounding these cultural and social goals for the body operate informally in schools. The formal bodily practices that occur in schools are concerned with controlling the appearance and behaviors of the individual and the social body. Together, these informal and formal bodily practices at the site of the school create what Kelly (1997) calls the invasive intimacy of the project of schooling: "Thronged corridors and classrooms, palpable threats, should more readily remind us that the territory of education is the body, and education territorializes the body" (p. 1).

Examining the body as the site of social and political control has been undertaken by scholars in diverse fields such as anthropology (Sault, 1994), education (Gore, 1993), and sociology (Kirk, 1993). Underneath the notion of the body as a site of social and political control is a vast network of power relationships. However, as Foucault (1980) cautions: "The individual is not a pre-given entity which is seized on by the exercise of power. The individual, with his identity and characteristics, is the product of a relation of power exercised over bodies" (p. 73). As will be shown in the next chapter, different levels and forms of power relationships, exercised in particular ways over, through, and in bodies, produce specific effects on the bodies of adolescent girls, constituting their bodies in particular ways.

But our identities cannot be kept separate from our bodies, says Bartky (1990).The constitution of the body is thus mutually interdependent with the constitution of the subject. Increasingly, according to Brumberg (1997), key questions of identity ("Who am I?" "Who do I want to be?") are being answered by adolescent girls in relation to their bodies. Statements made by the girls in this study such as "I'd like to have a body that makes me feel good about myself" (Raye: 06/04/98) and "If I were thinner I'd have it all" (Angela: 06/16/98) are examples of how girls experience the inseparability of identity and body.

The poststructural conception of identity is best able to account for the interconstituency of the mind and the body in the constitution of the subject. The subject is the individual in society (Belsey, 1980) and subjectivity, according to Weedon (1987, p. 32), refers to "the conscious and unconscious thoughts and emotions of the individual, her sense of self and her ways of understanding her relation to the world." Attention to the unconscious, as well as the conscious, in the constitution of identity is fundamental to the notion of subjectivity and is in opposition to the modernist notion of identity that is singular, rational, fully fixed and stable (Kelly, 1997). Following Kelly, I use the term "identity" not in the modernist sense; rather, I refer to the individual subject in society whose identity, or subjectivity, is constituted through social structures and through language (Davies, 1993). Here, identity is conceptualized as a process that develops in a matrix of structuring social and institutional relationships and practices (Davidson, 1996). This matrix of subject positions results from various discourses: "The displacement of subjectivity across a range of discourses implies a range of subject positions from which the subject grasps itself and its relations with the real" and these positions may be incompatible or contradictory (Belsey, 1980, p. 65). As the data will show, the participants in this study encountered a range of discourses, practices and power relationships in which their bodies (and hence their identities) were constituted.

Power

Maybe that's why the teacher doesn't like me, because I have so much power over her. I have a lot of power here. I control other students, and I can control teachers, and I can control my parents. (Angela: 12/10/98)

This statement suggests that Angela has conceived of power as an individual personality trait linked with the submission of others. This view of power is abundant in the literature, especially within the current literature on resistance that acknowledges the relationship between power and resistance. Sun's (1995) argument, that power hierarchies in schools and the resultant power conflicts and struggles between students and school authorities lead to student resistance, is found in virtually all accounts of student resistance (Epp, 1996; Everhart, 1983; Fine, 1991; Kohl, 1994; Miron & Lauria, 1995; Sefa Dei et al., 1997; Starr, 1981; Willis, 1977). These works implicate the asymmetrical power relations in the construction of resistance: "It has been recognized that the power structure of school has placed students not only at the bottom of the power hierarchy, but also in constant conflicts with their teachers, school, staff, and school administrators" (Sun, 1995, p. 843). The power structure of the school is not located historically, nor is it questioned. Lacking in these accounts is a theoretical grounding of the concept of power and a detailed analysis of the relationship between power and resistance. Largely, they are based on a repressive notion of power—that is, power is viewed as something to be wielded by one person, the teacher, in order to ensure the continued docility and submission of the students. Repressive power is used to dominate, oppress, coerce and deny. Focusing on one form of power conceals the presence of other relationships of power. In discussions of classroom power relationships that highlight an asymmetrical relationship between teachers and students, the webs of social relationships in the classroom and in the school are hidden.

I use Foucault's (1980) concepts of relational power and "regime of truth" as theoretical lenses through which to view power relations as they are constructed in particular classrooms and as they are experienced by particular students.* I agree with Bordo (1993) that much poststructuralist thought (the work of Foucault in particular) is better understood as "offering interpretive tools rather

---

* Feminists have both embraced and denounced Foucault's theory of power. It is not my intention to defend Foucault's theory of power but to acknowledge that this theory does not exist unproblematically. Many feminist writers have critiqued Foucault. They have argued that his theory is insufficient to the analysis of gender and the analysis of power relations that affect the lives of women (Allen, 1996; Bartky, 1990; Haber, 1996; Hartsock, 1990). Allen (1996), for example, argues that Foucault's focus on the micro-level analysis of power relations foregrounds particular oppressive

than theoretical frameworks for wholesale adoption" (p. 336). The merit to using regime of truth as an interpretive tool, according to Gore (1993), is the identification of previously unrecognized workings of power, such as those within the social webs of the classroom. The constitutive effects of power relationships and discourses on the bodies and subjectivities of adolescent girls in the contextual density of schooling can therefore be revealed. By looking at specific struggles of adolescent girls, I establish concretely the nature of these struggles as their bodies are constituted at school socially, culturally and institutionally.

Relational Power

According to Foucault (1980), power is something that circulates; it is never appropriated as a commodity; it is employed and exercised through a net-like organization; and individuals are always in the position of simultaneously being subject to and exercising power. In this view, power is relational: "In reality, power means relations, a more-or-less organized hierarchical co-ordinated cluster of relations" (Foucault, 1980, p. 198). Foucault (1987) says that relations of power constitute a complex field: "The relationships of power have an extremely wide extension in human relations. There is a whole network of relationships of power, which can operate between individuals, in the bosom of the family, in the political body, etc." (p. 3). At home, for example, in the "bosom of the family," young people may find their use of space and time subject to surveillance and control by adults (Skelton & Valentine, 1998). Relationships of power, then, can be found at different levels and under different forms. They are changeable, reversible and unstable (Foucault, 1987).

Foucault (1987) identifies three levels of relationships of power. Strategic relationships are the "games that result in the fact that some people try to determine the conduct of others" (Foucault, 1987, p. 19). The second level, techniques of government or governmental technologies, refers to "the way in which you govern your wife, your children, as well as the way you govern an institution" (Foucault,

---

relations between two individuals but ignores how these relations come to be. Although Foucault did not undertake a specific analysis of power relations that affect women, he clearly recognized that women are subjected to oppressive relations of power: "Women, prisoners, conscripted soldiers, hospital patients, and homosexuals have now begun a specific struggle against the particularized power, the constraints and controls, that are exerted over them" (Foucault, 1977, p. 216).

1987, p. 19). In a state of domination—the third level of power relationships—"the relations of power, instead of being variable and allowing different partners a strategy which alters them, find themselves firmly set and congealed" (Foucault, 1987, p. 3).

At any level, power exists only when it is put into action, says Foucault (1982a):

> The exercise of power is not simply a relationship between partners, individual or collective: it is a way in which certain actions modify others. Which is to say, of course, that something called Power, with or without a capital letter, which is assumed to exist universally in a concentrated or diffused form, does not exist. (p. 219)

In relationships of power at various levels, individuals or groups exercise power through actions, and relations of power can become fixed in such a way that they are perpetually asymmetrical (Foucault, 1987). Even when the relation of power is not equally balanced, the individual who is relatively powerless continues to have options for action against the powerful. For example, says Foucault (1987), the individual "still has the possibility of committing suicide, of jumping out the window or of killing the other" (p. 12).

Applied to the classroom, the concept of relational power allows for the identification and analysis of multiple forms and levels of power relationships in addition to the asymmetrical power relation between teacher and student. No longer can it be assumed that the teacher is the sole possessor of a universal and concentrated form of power in the classroom. Rather, educational institutions bring into play a whole series of power processes, including enclosure, surveillance, and reward and punishment (Foucault, 1982a). In addition to these forms of power that are exercised at the institutional level, other relationships of power can occur, because, as Foucault (1984) says, power is always present in human relations. As discussed previously, resistance to these forms of power is possible, because points of resistance are present everywhere in the power network (Foucault, 1976). In order to identify the network of relationships of power (and resistances) at the level of the classroom, I use Foucault's concept of regime of truth as a tool for analysis "so as to bring to light power relations, locate their position, find out their points of application, and the methods used" (1982a, p. 211).

Regimes/Games of Truth

Truth, according to Foucault (1980), "is linked in circular relations with systems of power which produce and sustain it, and to effects of power which it induces and which extend it" (p. 133). In a regime of truth, a particular relationship between truth and power is enacted through specific techniques and practices:

> Each society has its regime of truth, its "general politics" of truth: That is, the types of discourse which it accepts and makes function as true; the mechanisms and instances which enable one to distinguish true and false statements, the means by which each is sanctioned; the techniques and procedures accorded value in the acquisition of truth; the status of those who are charged with saying what counts as true (Foucault, 1980, p. 131).

Any given regime "designates the way in which the conduct of individuals or of groups might be directed: the government of children, of souls, of communities, of families, of the sick" (Foucault, 1982a, p. 221). Power, then, is a question of government, where governing is used in its broadest sense as a means of structuring the possible field of action of others (Foucault, 1982a). The field of actions structures and is structured by the discourses, techniques and practices (the "truth") of the regime.

The techniques and practices of a regime are "the means of bringing power relations into being" (Foucault, 1982a, p. 223). They may include more or less complex means of control, systems of surveillance, and "rules which are or are not explicit, fixed or modifiable" (Foucault, 1982a, p. 223). Later in his writing, Foucault (1987) distinguishes between two forms of techniques and practices of power: he describes practices of the self as "an exercise of self upon self by which one tries to work out, to transform one's self and to attain a certain mode of being" (p. 2). Other techniques of power are not directed to one's self; these are the techniques "in which one wants to direct the behavior of another" (Foucault, 1987, p. 11). The techniques and practices of power in a regime of truth, "the application of power over ourselves or others" (Foucault, 1982a, p. 224), are not instances of individual creativity:

> These practices are nevertheless not something that the individual in-
> vents by himself. They are patterns that he finds in his culture and which
> are proposed, suggested and imposed on him by his culture, his society,
> and his social group. (Foucault, 1987, p. 11)

The techniques and practices of power may also be referred to
as procedures. Foucault (1987) described games of truth in much
the same way as he described regime of truth: "When I say 'game,'
I mean an ensemble of rules for the production of truth. . . it is an
ensemble of procedures which lead to a certain result" (p. 16). Techniques, practices, or procedures that bring relationships of power
into being lead to certain results within particular regimes or games
of truth. This is not to say that the exercise of power is algorithmic
and fixed and that the techniques and practices of power lead always
to the same result. Creativity and imagination can emerge when
an individual begins a struggle against a particular form of power:
"modes of resistance are already modes of invention and modes of
escape" (Feher, 1987, p. 167). In response to the vast network of power relations, multiple forms of resistance are possible:

> There is a plurality of resistances, each of them a special case: resistances
> that are possible, necessary, improbable; others that are spontaneous,
> savage, solitary, concerted, rampant, or violent; still others that are quick
> to compromise, interested, or sacrificial; by definition, they can only ex-
> ist in the strategic field of power relations. (Foucault, 1975, p. 96)

Within any regime of truth, then, the identification of forms, techniques and practices of power will also illuminate the kinds of resistances that are possible.

Regime of truth is a concept that encompasses not only the relationship between power and truth but also describes their relationship to self. Gore (1993) describes Foucault's notion of self as
the ethical aspect of a regime of truth. Foucault (1987) noted that
relationships exist "between the constitution of the subject or different forms of the subject and games of truth, practices of power and
so forth" (p. 10). In particular, Foucault (1987) believed that subjects
actively constitute themselves through the specific practices of particular regimes of truth in order to attain certain modes of being. To
attain a certain mode, care for self is required:

One cannot care for self without knowledge. The care for self is of course knowledge of self... but it is also the knowledge of a certain number of rules of conduct or of principles which are at the same time truths and regulations. To care for self is to fit one's self out with these truths. That is where ethics is linked to the game of truth. (Foucault, 1987, p. 5)

Foucault applied regime of truth to societies, but according to Gore (1993) regime of truth can be applied at micro-levels of pedagogy as a concept and as a tool. As a concept, "Regime of truth can be applied to discourses and practices that reveal sufficient regularity to enable their immanent naming" (1993, p. 55).

Gore (1993) maintains that the classroom is an important site to see the actualization of a particular regime of truth because the pedagogical process embodies power relations between and among teachers and learners. The dominant school culture, or discourse, is one regime of truth actualized at the level of the classroom. The asymmetrical power relation that characterizes the teacher-student relationship is central to the regime of truth in the dominant school discourse. Another form of power to be found in schools is what Foucault calls "institutional power." Although Foucault did not write a detailed historical analysis of power relations in schools as he did of prisons and mental institutions, he repeatedly classifies schools with prisons, hospitals and barracks in his discussions of institutional power.* Within this conception of institutional power, power is not centered in any one individual: "One doesn't have here a power which is wholly in the hands of one person who can exercise it alone and totally over the others. It's a machine in which everyone is caught, those who exercise power just as much as those over whom it is exercised" (Foucault, 1980, p. 156).

The official institutional regime of truth, characterized by hierarchical relationships between teachers and students and the exercise of institutional power, is by no means the only regime experienced

---

* See, for example, "Generalized Punishment," "Docile Bodies," "The Means of Correct Training" and "Panopticism" in *Discipline and Punish* and "The Eye of Power," "Truth and Power," and "Prison Talk" in *Power/Knowledge.*

Foucault is not the only writer, nor the first, to compare schools to prisons. Jackson (1968) contended that schools resembled prisons in that "one subgroup of their clientele (the students) are involuntarily committed to the institution, whereas another subgroup (the staff) has greater freedom of movement and, most important, has the ultimate freedom to leave the institution entirely" (p. 31).

by students. At school, "Adolescents move among multiple and often competing rules and rituals of different contexts" (Finders, 1997, p. 18). The competing rules and rituals of different contexts can produce regimes of truth. Students find themselves "thrust into a network of practices of power and constraining institutions" (Foucault, 1987, p. 17). Hence, "the games (of truth) can be extremely numerous" (Foucault, 1987, p. 20).

Regime of truth, as an interpretive tool, is especially useful to the analytical framework because it highlights the relationship between power, discourse, social institutions, and subjectivity. In the next chapter, I use the key features of regime of truth (relations of power, techniques, practices and procedures that bring power relations into being, mode of being, and results or social effects of the practices) to identify and to discuss three regimes of truth that seem to be at play within the institution of schooling. Using Feher's (1987) definition, I refer to these regimes as regimes of the body. Each regime is concerned with the discipline, regulation, order and control of adolescent bodies, and each of them operates within the institution of the school, constituting not only bodies of determinate types but also particular forms of the subject.

sumption that adolescent girls are a homogeneous group. I attend to differences among the participants by including anecdotes that demonstrate the multiple and contradictory voices of adolescent girls. The task of interpretation is to bring out these living interweavings in their full, ambiguous, multivocal character (Jardine, 1998).

This analysis is based on the premise that the body is culturally, socially, and historically constituted (Grosz, 1994; Kirk, 1993; Sault, 1994). That is, particular kinds of bodies are produced within regimes of the body. In order to analyze the ways in which adolescent bodies are produced, I identify regimes of truth concerned with the discipline, regulation, order and control of adolescent bodies, individually and collectively. Using Feher's (1987) definition, I refer to these regimes as regimes of the body. Feher describes practices and techniques as a key feature of regimes of the body: "Power is real but relational; virtual, it needs to be actualized, and our bodies are the objects, the terms, of its relation. A certain combination of these relations of power—a certain promotion of practices and techniques—can be called a political regime of the body" (p. 159–160). Within the institution of schooling, then, I identify and analyze three regimes of the body:

1. An institutional regime that disciplines individual bodies and the social body institutionally—that is, through the use of techniques and procedures that are officially sanctioned,
2. A social regime that disciplines the social body through the power of the peer dynamic, and
3. A cultural regime that disciplines individual bodies according to dominant cultural definitions of femininity.

My concern in this study is with what I found to be current regimes of the body. This does not imply that I view regimes of the body as fixed and unchanging. In *The Body Project: An Intimate History of American Girls*, Brumberg (1997) provides an excellent historical analysis regarding the shifting ensemble of rules surrounding the female body. For example, Brumberg shows how menarche has become a hygienic crisis rather than a maturational event, much as it had been viewed by the Victorians.

Regime
of the Boc

The body is molded by a great many distinct regimes; it is broken (
by the rhythms of work, rest and holidays; it is poisoned by food or
ues, through eating habits or moral laws; it constructs resistances. (
cault, 1977, p. 153)

Introduction

ONE OF THE CRITICISMS OF FEMINIST POSTSTRUCTURAL
in education is that scholars have not yet concerned themsel
issues of schooling at a local level (Gore, 1993). I respond
criticism by grounding this analysis in particular practices a
level (a middle school and a junior high) and by providing
insights into who students are and how they see their world
Wilson, 1996). I attend to the specificities of context.

This chapter is not intended to provide a unifying accour
experiences of the girls. Rather, by providing phenomenolog
counts of multiplicity and contradiction (Gore, 1993) using e
from the girls' narratives, I hope to illustrate, among man
things, the poststructuralist insight that women's voices are r
in nature (Nicholson, 1999). I do not present the data under

As an interpretive tool, regime of truth is a useful construct well suited to this analysis. It allows exploration of the relationship between discourse, subjectivity, social institutions and power in the construction of adolescent bodies. It provides a position from which to ask what Gore (1993) describes as key poststructuralist questions:

1. Where are the regimes to be found?
2. How do they get produced and regulated?
3. How do they function? How are they enacted?
4. What are their social effects?

For the purposes of this analysis, I use the key features of regime of truth as discussed in chapter 5 (relations of power, techniques, practices and procedures that bring power relations into being, mode of being, and results or social effects of the practices) in order to respond to these key questions. Institutional, social, and cultural regimes of the body are discussed in terms of the power relationships inherent in each regime, the techniques that are utilized, the mode of being that is being constructed, and the effects of the regime on the lives of adolescent girls.

Representing the regimes of the body as separate and distinct regimes reduces their complexity and multiplicity, as the act of categorization is an act of simplification (Gore, 1993). It is not my intention to represent these regimes as discrete categories but to name the categories and then to displace them by offering contradictions both within and between the regimes. In the final section of the analysis, chapter 7, I demonstrate how the three regimes operate simultaneously and within the context of a particular class, physical education: these regimes "are superimposed, they cross, impose their own limits, sometimes cancel one another out, sometimes reinforce one another" (Foucault, 1987, p. 224).

Institutional Regime of the Body

Another stupid thing is the dress code rule. You're not allowed to show your belly button or your shoulders. Because teenage boys are going through hormones and they'll think something. That's a crock, that boys can't control their hormones. They can if they want to. But if something happened, they say it would be our fault. (Sheresa: 06/11/98)

I use the term institutional regime to describe the regime of the body that is officially sanctioned at the site of the school. It is a part of the institutional culture that seeks to coordinate the conduct of individual students to express the collective values to which individuals in the organization subscribe (Clifton & Roberts, 1993). The coordination of individual bodies into the student body links the singular and the multiple, or what Foucault (1975) calls the first of the great operations of discipline: transforming the confused, useless or dangerous multitudes into ordered multiplicities. In the institutional regime of the body, individual and collective bodies are manipulated by authority (Foucault, 1975) through a number of rules and regulations intended to produce docile bodies and ordered multiplicities. In fact, schooling is the means by which particular forms of subjectivity and particular forms of participation in social life are produced (Kelly, 1997). However, the production of docile bodies is not simply a one-way, cause-and-effect relationship between the institution and individual students. Resistance, as we have seen, is always possible within any relationship of power. Although individuals are capable of resistance to particular techniques of power, at times, especially when the relationship of power is asymmetrical, the margin of liberty may be extremely limited (Foucault, 1987). Many of the girls in this study perceived that they were relatively powerless in the face of institutional power: "There's not much students can do about all the rules. What's the point?" (Alicia: 03/12/98). But at other times, participants expressed their pleasure in being able to fool the institution. Even though they were relatively powerless, the girls thought of elaborate schemes to bypass or mock the school rules.

Student bodies may be manipulated into docile bodies through two levels and forms of relationships of power within the institution of schooling: a macro-level and a micro-level. At both of these levels, power is experienced in its capillary form, or "the point where power reaches into the very grain of individuals, touches their bodies and inserts itself into their actions and attitudes, their discourses, learning processes and everyday life" (Foucault, 1980, p. 36). The macro and micro levels of power were experienced by the girls.

The macro-level of power relationships refers to the background of specific relations. The background of the teacher-student relationship is located within the realm of institutional power, as outlined in chapter 5. Institutional power is what Foucault (1987) calls the second level of power relationships, referring to the way an institution is governed. It is described by Foucault as the "machine of power." The machine of institutional power is experienced as faceless, nameless, and, often, ludicrous. It is difficult to hold one individual accountable for institutional rules; instead criticisms are more broadly directed, to "them" or to the "school." Alicia's comments illustrate the experience of institutional power as ludicrous and generally dispersed throughout the school:

> Don't be offended but this school is such a hole. It really is. Part of what makes it such a hole is that there's so many rules and they're just dumb. Some of the rules are so juvenile it's pointless. Like the back-pack rule: no back-packs in the hall. It's pointless. It would make more sense for them to apply the rules not to everybody but just to the people who need them. Like when the bathrooms were locked because of the fires. That was dumb because it wasn't everybody that was doing it, just one or two people. (03/12/98)

The micro-level, on the other hand, refers to power relationships between individuals. One such form of power, a strategic relationship, occurs when one person tries to determine the conduct of other people (Foucault, 1987). The teacher-student relationship can often take this form:

> It just bugs me how the teachers think they have control over our lives, over every little thing that you do. Most of my teachers, they're like, "You have to do it this certain way and if you don't then you're just going to get punished for it. They're always bugging you to get your work done: "You have to get this done or else you're going to have to suffer the consequences." (Raye, 11/04/98)

The macro and micro power relationships reinforce one another (Foucault, 1982a) and make possible the exercise of discipline upon the bodies of students. At the site of the school, asymmetrical teacher-student power relationships are grounded within institutional power. One of the ways that the girls experienced the integration of macro and micro power was when teachers became the enforcers of school rules.

Yet teachers, too, are caught in the machine of power. At the Creekwood site, for example, many teachers were just as frustrated as the students when the student washrooms remained locked. Most students, however, perceived the teachers as rule-makers and enforcers. They assumed that the teachers agreed with the rules that had been formulated outside of their classrooms. In other words, the students experienced the play of institutional power as a form of micro-level power. That is, teachers were the agents of the institution. Only one participant, Angela, seemed to recognize that teachers were also caught in the machine of power. She insisted that it was not the teachers' fault when they had to enforce school rules and regulations (02/24/98).

Producing Docile Bodies and Ordered Multiplicities

Within the institutional regime of the body, the goal, or mode of being, of the techniques and practices of power is the production of docile bodies, individually and as ordered multiplicities. A docile body, as Foucault (1975) notes, is one that may be subjected, used, transformed, and improved, and the process of schooling plays a key role in producing appropriately compliant yet useful bodies (Kirk, 1993). The regime of the body at the institutional level is concerned largely with regulating bodies in space, articulating the ways in which bodies accomplish certain tasks and the ways that bodies may relate to one another. For example, teachers draw on the institutionalized authority of their official positions to claim the right to regulate the students' activities, movement, posture, talking, possessions, access to water, and time and manner of eating (Thorne, 1993). Techniques and practices of power in the institutional regime are enacted at the site of the body—through rules, regulations, and school policies.

Many of the rules and regulations in the school are governed by the naturalized discourse of adolescence. Adolescent bodies, characterized by physical and hormonal changes, are objectified as things that are out of control (Lesko, 1996). The naturalized discourse of adolescence is one example of how common-sense, taken-for-granted ideas are inscribed in an institutional discourse. According to Lesko, the reigning conception of the adolescent is that of a natural being, universal and historical, with certain immutable characteristics. In this view, human subjectivity is reduced to one dimension: age. An assumption underlying this conception is the belief that adolescents are controlled by hormones. Language plays an important role in naturalizing this conception of adolescence: "Because it is characteristic of language to be overlooked, the differences it constructs may seem to be natural, universal and unalterable when in reality they may be produced by a specific form of a social organization"(Belsey, 1980, p. 42). In other words, common-sense notions of adolescence are constructed by a discourse that uses language to differentiate between adults and adolescents. Lesko maintains that the scientific view of adolescence contributes to a series of binary oppositions (adult/adolescent, body/mind, massed/individuated) and that "People between the ages of 12 and 17 years are believed to naturally and inevitably possess certain characteristics and behaviors that correspond with essentially different natures than those of adults" (p. 155). Adolescents are assigned inferior status within schools and beyond the boundaries of schools. Within this naturalized discourse of adolescence, students are positioned in school and in society in general as "out of control." The stereotypical definition of teenagers knows no boundaries, as Emma reports:

> Everyone, including the teachers, thinks that teenagers are bad. Like in stores, people think teenagers are dangerous because they steal. There are signs that say "Only three teenagers at a time are allowed in." Probably adults steal more than teenagers. But teenagers have the bad reputation. (06/15/98)

Rules and Regulations

The assumptions that undergird adolescence directly shape the development of rules, regulations and policies at the school. When adolescents are viewed as being naturally out of control, authorities assume they require a multitude of rules to control them. The resulting micropenality is "a kind of judicial privilege, with its own laws, its specific offenses, its particular forms of judgement" (Foucault, 1975, p. 193). At the Creekwood site, the specific offenses and the form of judgement attached to each offense is called the "Discipline Cycle." Gum chewing, for example, was an offense. The form of judgement attached to gum chewing was dependent upon the number of times a student had been caught chewing gum. For a first offense, the student is asked to spit out her gum. A second offense results in writing lines, and a third offense, now considered to be defiance, has a harsher penalty. A student caught chewing gum a third time has to spend the lunch hour in a detention room and her parents are informed (Field notes: 09/12/98). This kind of disciplinary program is an example of the perpetual penality that supervises every instant in the disciplinary institution (Foucault, 1975). As will be seen in chapter 7, the Discipline Cycle is based on a model of moral understanding that requires students (and teachers) to assume fixed and unitary subject positions.

The micropenality of a school disciplinary system that attempts to make "children's bodies the object of highly complex systems of manipulation and conditioning" (Foucault, 1980) relies on surveillance as a technique of power. The supervision of the smallest fragment of life and body (Foucault, 1975) becomes necessary in order to produce docile bodies and ordered multiplicities: bodies that pay attention in class, bodies that sit quietly during instruction, and bodies that walk down hallways in an orderly fashion. The gaze of the teacher is a disciplinary technique used to ensure that the rules of conduct are followed by students.

The naturalized discourse of adolescence becomes institutionalized through the rules and regulations of a particular school. School policies integrate other discourses of the body found beyond the school culture along with the naturalized discourse of adolescence. Policies such as dress codes serve to reinforce dominant discourses of the body, making them function as if they are true. It is often the case, says Kelly (1997) that schools, rather than disarming such discourses, "proceed as if these subject positions are *givens* requiring compensatory measure" (p. 100). She gives the example of "Women are victims; we must learn to protect ourselves." At the level of the school, the dress code is an example of the cultural myth of woman as victim and as sexual temptress (Bordo, 1993). In this discourse, women are seen as continually and actively luring men to arousal, and the arousal of men's desires is the result of female manipulation and is the woman's fault (Bordo, 1993). This is reflected within Sheresa's comments at the beginning of the chapter. A school dress code policy that works to conceal certain parts of the female body (e.g., shoulders and belly buttons) is correctly interpreted by students as the institution's attempt to restrict the girls from arousing the boys, for their own protection—an attempt they feel is unfounded. When discussing her school's dress policy, Sheresa notes that boys can control their hormones if they want to (Interview: 06/11/98). She goes on to say that if "something" happens (an unwanted sexual advance), "they say that it would be our fault." A school's dress code policy primarily affects the bodies of the female students, a double standard that did not go unnoticed by the girls: "The dress code is about what the girls can and can't wear. The boys can wear whatever they want. It's not fair. If we wear certain things, then we're sluttish. But the boys are never sluttish" (Emma: 06/15/98).

Rules, regulations, and policies that regulate the conduct, comportment and appearance of adolescent bodies comprise the techniques and practices of the institutional regime of the body. The goal or mode of being, of this regime is the production of docile bodies and organized multiplicities in order to prevent the chaos that would surely ensue if these unruly bodies were left in their natural state. The institution integrates power relations at a micro-level (the teacher-student relationship) and a macro-level (institutional power) in order to produce compliant, yet useful, bodies. But in the face of these relations of power, a whole field of responses, reactions, results, and possible inventions may open up (Foucault, 1982a). The next section describes the ways in which the girls responded to the institutional regime of the body.

Responses, Reactions, Results, Inventions

Erickson (1987) maintains that students experience an illegitimate and oppressive system within the institution of schooling:

> The more alienated the students become, the less they persist in doing their school work. Thus they fall farther and farther behind in academic achievement. The student becomes actively resistant—seen as salient and incorrigible—or passively resistant—fading into the woodwork as an anonymous, well-behaved, low-achieving student. (p. 348)

In contrast to this either/or position, the girls in this study demonstrated wider variety in the field of responses to the institutional regime. They often complied with many of the rules, regulations and policies. At other times, the girls actively or passively resisted the demands of their teachers and the institution. In some of these instances, the girls were not merely negating the rule of the institution; they were actively creating a different game of truth. And many times, although they appeared to be complying, the girls were resisting in the backstage regions of the classroom.

COMPLIANCE AND THE APPEARANCE OF COMPLIANCE The girls often complied with direct teacher demands for conduct and comportment (e.g., turn around, sit still, put up your hand if you have something to say, line up at the door, etc.). In the absence of direct teacher demands, the participants would often continue to obey the rules of conduct. Part of the process of schooling, in addition to being managed, involves students learning to manage themselves. Gore (1993) refers to this process as self-disciplining where students keep themselves and others in check. August admonishing her friends ("Shut up. I'm listening to the teacher") is an example of self-disciplining (Field notes: 05/13/98). Individual students attempting to keep themselves in check may have interiorized the teacher's gaze. That is, students become responsible for exercising surveillance over themselves in the same ways that their teachers might, as Foucault (1980) notes:

> There is no need for arms, physical violence, material constraints. Just a gaze. An inspecting gaze, a gaze which each individual under its weight will end by interiorizing to the point that he is his own overseer, each individual thus exercising this surveillance over, and against, himself. (p. 155)

Students may appear to have docile bodies—that is, they comply with teacher expectations for behavior and academic work. The appearance of compliance does not necessarily indicate a docile body, however, as this student account demonstrates:

> It was a project that I really didn't want to do. It was a social project that we had been working on. And the teacher just talked forever, she just talked, the same thing over and over again and we never got any time to actually get down to work. We had double social class, and it was "No, I'm not going. I can't do this anymore. It's a waste of my time. I'm going to work on my project at home instead of going to school. I can get a lot more done." And that morning I did. I got my project almost completely

finished. She talked all morning from what I heard. She did exactly what we thought she would do. And I got an excellent grade on my project. (Angela: 12/10/98)

In this example, Angela conceals her unruly body from her teacher. Because Angela completes her project (without getting caught for skipping school) and exceeds the criteria for success, her teacher continues to believe that Angela is a docile body. In other cases, students did not attempt to conceal their lack of compliance:

Sometimes I don't bother doing an assignment because it's not worth your time. Like this thing in Humanities. I'm not going to do that. She wants a retelling of a story that she read to us a week ago that we have to rewrite. Like I'm going to remember all of that. What's the point? (Sheresa: 06/11/98)

Refusing to comply, then, can be another response to the demand for becoming a docile body.

BREAKING RULES Another response in the field of possible responses to the institutional regime of the body occurs as a reaction to the micropenality in the school—the multitude of rules and regulations interpreted by some students as juvenile and pointless. Alicia explains why she, and her friends, are compelled to actively break rules:

People just don't like authority, especially here at school. Here, we're not really listened to because we're just stupid little kids, right? So we break all the rules because there are too many and we're trying to push them back because we want to be treated fair. (03/12/98)

In this example, breaking rules can be seen as an anti-authority move, as breaking rules for the sake of breaking rules. As Alicia notes, thought, breaking rules can also be interpreted as refusal to accept the identity assigned by the school, that of a "stupid little kid" and a docile body.

CREATION In addition to the various forms of acceptance, or resistance, to the production of a docile body, students are also capable of creating an alternative learning environment within the classroom. In any regime of truth, according to Foucault (1987), there is always the possibility to discover something else, to more or less change the rules, and even the totality of the regime. Applying Bakhtin's (1968) notion of carnival, building a second world and a second life outside officialdom, shows how students create an alternative social context within the classroom. Carnival, the people's second life, is organized on the basis of laughter (Bakhtin, 1968). This playful stance to the world was demonstrated by the girls when they mocked the school's rules and regulations and teased the teachers (and the researcher). Alicia, for example, wrote humorous notes, developing an inside joke with me about my upcoming demise ("Dear Ms. Olafson: Just in case you don't die, and we've already spent all your money on a toothpick, you could try selling these Happy Meal Toy ideas to McDonalds"). Practices such as these are fun, and create a different context within the institutional regime. Creating fun is necessary in the context of being at school, according to Raye: "You do all that stuff to have fun. That's the reason for living. If you never had any fun then your life is going to be miserable" (11/25/98). The officialdom of the school is perceived as being not fun; therefore students create their own forms of enjoyment. Another game to be played is skipping school. As noted previously in chapter 2, Angela describes skipping as a game: "It's all a game. I'm enjoying it. It's fun to get away with things and still pull off the marks" (12/10/98). Here Angela also alludes to the pleasure derived from playing these games and remaining undetected. Foucault (1976) refers to this sense of enjoyment as "the pleasure that kindles at having to evade this power, flee from it, fool it, or the travesty of it" (p. 45). "Fooling" the institutional regime was indeed a source of pleasure for the girls. Although the "margins of liberty" appear to be limited within the institution of schooling, many students attempted to open up spaces for resistance.

Social Regime of the Body

In Grade Six I tried to kill myself because I thought that everyone hated me. Everyone made fun of me. There was this one person who was popular and I wanted her to like me, and she was like, "You know, you're so annoying, you're really ugly, you're such a bitch, it's no wonder everyone hates you." And I was devastated. (Raye: 06/19/98)

The social regime of the body is part of the social system that peers create for themselves (Ruiz, 1998). The relations that students form among them creates what Ruiz (1998) maintains is a complex and virtually unknown system. The experiences of the girls in this study certainly support Ruiz's claim of a complex system. As Raye notes, this peer-created social system can have a significant impact on students' lives.

Modes of Being

The need for acceptance and the desire for popularity are cited by many adolescent girls as overwhelming concerns (Maracek & Arcuri, 1995; Debold, 1995; Dyer & Tiggemann, 1996). In fact, "Girls in grades six and seven rate being popular and well-liked as more important than being competent or independent" (AAUW Report, 1992, p. 11). This sentiment was echoed by Raye, who generated this definition of success at school on the student goal section of her report card: "I want to be accepted to the popular group" (Field notes: 12/02/98). Instead of writing an academic goal, which was the intended purpose for including a student goal section, Raye's desire for popularity takes precedence over grades. Success at middle school is measured by popularity, not by academic achievement.

Distressingly for some though, the criteria for popularity are not stable across school sites, nor do they remain constant within a school. Brenda noted that in her previous school she had been popular, but when she moved to another town this was no longer the case:

> Being popular is different in different schools. In my old school I was popular and then I moved here and I wasn't. That was really hard. I don't know why, because I look right and stuff and I'm nice. Here, I'm the middle class. Definitely. I'm not way off. (11/25/98)

Angela described the changes in criteria for popularity from grade to grade, noting that in grade 5 it was important to be short, skinny and blonde and by grade 8 the expectations had changed to perfection, which she defined as being pretty, getting good marks in school, and being in the right places with the right people (03/28/99). However, perfection can also have its price, especially if you are perceived as too perfect:

> When Penny came to our school she had the nicest clothes, the nicest hair, the best body. She's really pretty. But they hated it because she was better than them. She was too perfect and so they didn't like it. But she was actually really nice. Now she's a Loser to some people, but she just went off and made her own little group. (Brenda 11/25/98)

The girls in this study aspired to be accepted: "My biggest fear is not getting accepted," said Raye (11/04/98). But acceptance and popularity do not have stable meanings within schools or between schools, and this was often a source of tension and confusion for the girls, especially because acceptance and popularity are related to membership in particular social groups at school. In her study of junior high school girls, Finders (1997) observed that the girls in the classroom she was studying formed two friendship groups, the social queens and the tough cookies. Similar to Finders's (1997) findings I observed separate, clearly bounded and hierarchical friendship groups at both research sites. However, unlike Finders, I observed a greater number of social groups, and I noted that the boundaries of these groups were fluid and that groups were regularly formed and disbanded. Angela described the instability of the social groups using a computer metaphor: "The social groups at school are like a screen saver—little spots fade, get brighter, change color. It's always shifting and moving" (06/16/98). The shifting, moving social groups in addition to the instability of the criteria for popularity mean that the social context at school experienced by the girls was fraught with tensions.

Hierarchical Friendship Groups

At the Creekwood site, there were a number of friendship groups. During one of our focus groups (05/22/98) the girls drew a web of these groups and categorized the various groups as having high, middle, and low status. Here, Brenda explains her interpretation of the social groups:

> The Popular group is probably the biggest group and they hang out with the guys and they all dress cool. I'm not really one of them. They group together. There's some people in the Popular group that you can't associate with unless you're with another popular person. They're total jerks. There's sections of the popular group—I think about four or five.

The Pathetic Wannabes are the people who follow the popular people around. Like Jean, she follows them around and everybody hates her, and everybody talks behind her back. They say such mean things. She just really wants to be cool and she thinks "If I stick with them long enough, they're going to like me," but they're really starting to hate her even more. And then there's the Skids. I think of them as Druggies because I know they have done drugs. They would be in the middle, between Losers and the Popular group. The Loser group is really quiet and they don't care about sports, they don't try to get into any activities and they're very judgmental. They really stick together. I don't really know them. I don't talk to them at all and they don't want to talk to me. They would probably ignore me anyhow. I think it's because people are rude to them and they think you're going to be mean to them even if you just walk up to them. The Loser group's fashions are hideous. They're awful. (Brenda: 11/25/98)

Disagreement existed among the participants regarding the labeling of these groups and their membership, illustrating how multiple ways of understanding the world arise from different circumstances (Eisenhart, 1998). In the following example, Rebecca uses a negative term to describe the popular group and she rejects Brenda's claim that she and her friends are Druggies:

And then there's a large range of people that are different from everyone else in the school that I would classify as Independents. They're people who have friends in school but they don't care if they're popular or not. Like me, I'm just here for the work. I'm not really into the social scene here—these are not the people I socialize with. We call the Popular group the Snob Squad. They think we're Druggies. I don't know why. We hang around with people that don't go to this school and some of them are Druggies but I don't know how they would know that. I don't know where they got the idea to call us Druggies. Maybe because we're not trying to socialize with them. We're not Druggies. (Rebecca: 02/17/99)

But according to Alicia, only two groups existed in the school: those who thought they were cool but really were not and those who were cool but nobody realized they were cool. She described the people who thought they were cool (the Popular group) as "so un-open-minded that it's not even funny. They think 'If you don't act like me, talk like me, and dress like me then you're not cool. You suck'" (03/12/98). By Alicia's definition, the only cool people were the Independents.

Disagreement was also apparent as students classified themselves as belonging to specific social groups. All of the participants agreed that Angela was very popular, although she identified herself as belonging to a subgroup of the popular people known as the Powerful group. Raye believed that she had finally been accepted into the Popular group ("I'm finally popular now and I'm so happy"), a claim that was disputed by another participant on the very same day: "Raye is in the Loser group, not the really really Loser group. But she's always following the popular people around" (Brenda: 11/25/98).

The social groups at Creekwood did not remain stable as the girls moved from grade seven to grade eight. Changes were precipitated by the departure and arrival of certain students:

> The Religious group from last year is gone. The main person for that group is being home-schooled this year, and so they just fell apart and joined different groups. There's a new group this year that didn't exist last year. It's called the Powerful group. One new kid changed the whole dynamic. The Powerful group can do anything; we control all the popular people. We float among the other groups. Like we can hang with Jocks or with the Popular people. But we have more personality, more brains and we're more socially in tune than anyone else. (Angela: 12/03/98)

Super Popular, Powerful, Popular, Snob Squad, Skids/Druggies, Independents, Pathetic Wannabes, Losers and Loners: these are the unstable and hierarchical social groups that organize the lives of adolescent girls. As Angela says, "Nobody really cares about the teachers and what they have to say. What happens at school, our actions, are determined by what's happening socially" (03/28/99). Students are labeled and assigned membership (by other students) to a particular group almost from the moment they walk into a school. The most important criterion is appearance: "At school, everything is based on your appearance. If a new person comes, they're first judged on what they look like and what they're wearing" (Sheresa: 06/08/98). Someone with hideous fashion, defined by Brenda as "stretch pants that go around your feet and the pants that go tight at the bottom," for example, would be assigned to a Loser group. However, a new student might also receive a "grace period," a period of time in which to prove herself prior to categorization:

> If you just move to the school, first off, they'll put you on trial and see if you pass everything. They'll try all these subtle tests that you encounter every single day of your life, so you don't notice it. If you do one thing wrong, they're like, "Well, she's weird," and then they're a little more cautious. But if you blow it too many times, you're out. They won't even talk to you. (Raye: 11/25/98)

The concept of positioning seems to be at work here, as the girls defined themselves and others as belonging to particular social groups. Positioning, largely a conversational process, is "the discursive practice whereby selves are located in conversations as observably and subjectively coherent participants in jointly produced story lines" (Davies & Harre, 1990, p. 48) The dynamics of social positioning are explained by Ellsworth (1997) using the analytical concept of mode of address from film study. Mode of address is a questioning about how the dynamics of social positioning get played out, and who you are addressed to be within networks of power relations associated with race, sexuality, gender and class. Each time we address someone, we take up a position within knowledge, power, and desire and assign to them a position in relation to ourselves and to a context (Ellsworth, 1997). Within the social regime of the body, students are assigned positions, often brutally, relative to their social acceptability, which they may accept or reject.

Techniques and Practices

In the public spaces of the school and within the classroom, a regime of the body that is socially constructed by the students' functions through the use of specific techniques and practices. The hierarchical social groups formed by the students become the basis of a system of techniques and practices. The complexity of this system is described by one of the girls:

> I find it very difficult to describe the social patterns of our school. I have decided that it can't be fully understood unless it is experienced. It seems very simple at first, but there are a least a million of the "unwritten" rules of social webbing that make it exceedingly complex. It starts out like this: you hang around with people who have common interests as you.

> There are not many of these large groups to choose from. From there it
> gets very complicated. A lot of stereotyping and politics comes into play.
> You may like the people you end up with, but it is very hard to beat this
> system. (Angela: 04/2/98)

The girls, as members of various hierarchical social groups,
spent a great deal of time and effort employing various strategies
of inclusion and exclusion to mark the boundaries of their particular groups. Verbal and physical strategies for exclusion ranged from
subtle (brushing off, acting bored) to overt (comments and actions).
It was surprising to me that the participants regarded these social
practices, recurrent categories of talk and action, as unremarkable
and as normal and undramatic features of everyday life (Lofland &
Lofland, 1995). The hierarchical social groups, often referred to as
cliques, are the informal groups that weave their way through larger
and more formal organizations, binding their members in invisible
but powerful ways (Lofland & Lofland, 1995). While I agree that
members are bound in powerful ways, I argue that members exclude
others in powerful ways and that the techniques and practices for
inclusion and exclusion are not "invisible." Rather, they have been
undetected by teachers and other school officials. For example, Raye
reports how a student in her class is very sneaky about bugging her:

> He always picks on my bad things. He doesn't see that I actually have
> something going for me. He says stuff like, "Don't you ever take a show-
> er?" and he picks on my peer social abilities. When I say something to
> the teacher, he puts on this complete innocent act, but as soon as her
> back is turned he starts making comments all over again. (11/04/98)

In this example, the student who is bugging Raye does so only
when the teacher's gaze is momentarily absent. Other forms of verbal and psychological ill-treatment, such as insults, threats, ridicul-
ing, social isolation, malicious gossip, petty theft and damage to personal belongings, are reported by Ruiz (1998) to be experienced by
25–35% of students. Much of this type of behavior happens when a
teacher's gaze is temporarily absent, making it nearly impossible to
detect. The social regime flourishes, primarily outside the teacher's
area of supervision in the public spaces of the school—the corridors,
lunchrooms, entrances and restrooms. Even when these areas are

supervised by teachers, verbal and psychological ill-treatment remains undetected. The teacher-supervisor cannot be everywhere at once, and oftentimes, as I observed at Creekwood, only one teacher may be supervising the public spaces during the lunch hour. During class times, the corridors were not supervised. According to Devine (1996) this means that the network of gazes has collapsed in the public spaces of the school, and students are now abandoned to one another's gazes. Yet verbal and psychological ill-treatment also occurs within classrooms, "offstage" (Finders, 1997) and hence also undetected. At the Kingwood site I recorded the following comments made by students towards one another within a span of only a few minutes (Field notes: 03/11/98):

> S1: Go away. You scare me. You have white things in your hair.
> S2: Eww. Look what she's wearing.
> S3: At least she has the guts to wear it.
> S4: I think you're gay or something.
> S5: Who, me?
> S4: No, your mom.

On another occasion, I observed that one of the girls was called a "skanky-ass whore" by a peer (in class, unheard by the teacher). August was surprised by my reaction, telling me that it was "nothing" and that more offensive terms are often used. She also noted, though, that she was not immune to the effects of name-calling: "They think they're not hurting your feelings, but it really hurts, you know?"(Field notes: 06/08/98).

Verbal and psychological ill-treatment, occurring in the public spaces of the school and within classrooms, is a form of exclusion. Forms of exclusion vary between social groups, according to Brenda:

> The different groups have different ways of excluding. Like the Loser group. I don't blame them actually, because we're all jerks. Every one of us has said something mean to them, I'll admit it. But they're seriously resenting. They're mean to others because nobody likes them. They'll say something first, and then you say it back. They start it, but I know that it's not really their fault. The Popular group does the brush-off, the cold shoulder. They usually just sort of walk off. And they stand in

a circle a lot to keep people out. And they never say something to your face; it's always behind your back. (11/25/98)

Meanness seemed to be an exclusionary tactic that occurred within all of the social groups at both research sites. Although Brenda insisted that the Popular group was not mean, Angela disagreed: "They aren't mean to the not-so-popular people because they don't really care about them. Internally, they're mean—vicious and backstabbing" (12/03/98). In addition to this kind of verbal meanness, the participants at the Kingwood site discussed forms of meanness that directly involved the physical body. Sheresa explains how a group of girls attacked her: "Girls can be mean. When I came back to school after being suspended, five chicks jumped me. They thought I was giving them dirty looks, that I was having problems with them. I had to get stitches on my eyebrow" (06/11/98).

Although the supervisory gaze of teachers and school staff may be absent or averted, students are not freed from the weight of surveillance in the public spaces of the school or within their own classrooms. As Currie (1999) notes, "The power of peers to affix the labels that determine social acceptability means that girls (as well as boys) are subject to continual assessment by their peers" (p. 244). Being under surveillance by peers may be even more brutal than the teacher's surveillance, and Angela describes continuous surveillance as "everyone's watching." She goes on to say, "But the worst is your classmates, because you want to be accepted. And even the Losers are watching you, too, because they want to be like you" (12/03/98). Everyone is indeed watching.

It is important to note that the techniques and practices of the social regime are not necessarily invented by the participants. Although the technique known as the grace period, for example, is particular to one of the school sites (Creekwood), it is an example of a pattern that has been imposed by culture, society and social group (Foucault, 1987). Techniques of inclusion and exclusion are not the exclusive domain of adolescent girls. These patterns are, perhaps, reflections of a larger narrative, according to Gilligan, Lyons and Hanmer (1990): "Girls' experiments in inclusion and exclusion—the tortuous clique formations through which girls may discover how it feels to be left out and what it means to be taken in—may provide a kind of dumbshow or dark mirroring of the adult world that girls are seeing" (p. 11). Although the girls may be creative in their formulations of patterns of inclusion and exclusion, they are patterns that they have inherited.

Effects

The social regime of the body, constituted through the power of the peer dynamic (Finders, 1997) in techniques and practices such as various forms of exclusion and surveillance, opens up a field of responses from the participants. These responses have a significant impact on everyday life at school.

WATCHFULNESS The instability of the social groups and continual assessment by one's peers mean that students must be careful not to disrupt the social order:

> The only thing I don't like about being popular is that you never know when your life is going to change. Because you can even look at somebody wrong and the next day you're going to be the most hated person in the entire school. You have to be really careful about what you say, how you say it, and who you say it to. You have to have a quick thinking mind. You have to know what's going on and then you have to quickly analyze it in your head. You have to read the situation. (Raye: 11/25/98)

The pressure to be socially accepted is a particular concern for those students trying to reach their goal of popularity. It is no easy task, as Angela explains: "If I moved to another school I'd have to start over. I'd have to start at the bottom of the social thing and work my way up" (06/16/98). Many students invest time and energy in "working their way up," changing their clothes and even their personalities:

> I'm definitely having a better year in terms of being accepted. It changed at the beginning of the year. I sort of changed my attitude and I changed my outlook on life and I just changed a lot about my personality. With my new personality, of course, I had to update my clothes, so I bought some new stuff. It's kind of more in and relaxed, just like my new personality. (Raye: 11/25/98)

Clearly, the girls spent a great deal of time at school observing the ever-changing dynamics of the social scene and trying to figure out where and how to belong.

REFUSAL Other students may refuse to accept the dominant ideas of what it means to be popular and accepted. The Independents (Alicia, Rebecca and Diane) at the Creekwood site and Sheresa (Kingwood) are examples of girls who did not enter into the social game of truth constructed by their peers. They were not outside the game; rather, they did not play by the same set of rules. Alicia explains the tensions she experienced when she chose not to accept the group's definition of popularity:

> I tried to dress like them one time. I went shopping and I tried on the clothes and I was just standing looking in the mirror thinking, "I look like them." But then I thought, "I don't want to be like them," so I didn't buy the stuff. Everybody wants to be the same, look the same. But that's stupid because not everybody thinks the same, not everybody acts the same, why should we dress the same? They're only saying that they feel bad about themselves so they want to get the attention off themselves onto somebody else so they don't feel bad. They're just insecure. I just learned not to cheat myself, not to care what they think. (05/28/98)

Alicia was seduced by the appeal of being popular and she learned that it was easy to change her appearance in order to be more like the Popular Group. But she also realized that she would have been selling herself out. However, the pressures of looking good and fitting in became overwhelming for many of the girls, including Alicia with her strong sense of self. Often, they chose to stay at home as a means to avoid the social regime:

> There's a different kind of freedom if you stay at home and don't go to school because you don't have to worry about what you're wearing, if your clothes match or if they're the right ones or whatever. Not like I'm really worried about that stuff but you just never have to worry about it all if you stay home to do your work. More than the hassle of coming to school, it's the hassle of everybody being stupid around you. There's always some argument or gossip or childish crap going around. You can't learn with people being stupid around you. For example, Karen came up to me and said, "Carol had done this and this to me, will you hate her with me?" I'm like, "Shut up. I'm not here to hate people." It's frus-

trating. It's just pathetic and pointless because tomorrow she's her best friend again. So it's meaningless too. Sometimes I feel like an outsider on the inside. I feel like I'm more mature than everybody else sometimes. (Alicia: 05/25/98)

Not participating in the dominant games of the social regime ("being an outsider on the inside"), resisting the pull to be the same, and maintaining a strong voice may be impossible within the school. For her grade 8 year, Alicia chose to be home-schooled. She felt this was the best solution for avoiding what she described as the hassles of everyone being stupid around her. Diane also chose home schooling midway through her grade eight year. Her decision was precipitated by the fact that her best friend, Rebecca, had been moved to another class. Rebecca explained that Diane found it impossible to continue in that classroom:

> She needs a friend to stick up for her and stuff. With two you can stand alone, but with one you can't. She can't stick up for herself by herself. You need backup to stick up for yourself. They make fun of her all the time. Put-downs, mean comments. They make fun of her ears because they're big. They make fun of her hair because even when she combs it it looks messy. (12/10/1998)

In Diane's case, the social regime effectively drove her from the school that made her feel miserable (Field notes: 01/21/99). Alicia, on the other hand, seemed to view her decision very positively, as an act of agency. These similar incidents, interpreted very differently by Diane and Alicia, again point to the possibility of multiple interpretations and the danger of assigning a single meaning to a particular event.

Achievement It is difficult to be academically successful at school when you are at the bottom of the social order. As one participant noted, "If everybody likes you, you're going to do well. If nobody likes you, you do bad" (Raye: 06/19/98). The girls were also concerned about how they, and their work, would be judged by their peers:

> I'm always worried about what the other kids are going to think of my work—if they're going to think I'm dumb or if they're going to like me any better if I do a really good job on my work. (Raye: 11/04/98)

Rebecca and Diane refused to do oral presentations in front of the class. Refusal meant escaping the continual assessment of them and their work by their peers. Alicia also engaged in this practice:

> I refuse to do oral presentations. You just worry that you're going to sound really stupid in front of the whole class. If you're stressed out you can't do as good a job because you're too worried about what people are going to think. (05/28/98)

Rebecca, Diane and Alicia skipped class if they were scheduled to do oral presentations. They preferred the consequences of skipping, ranging from receiving a grade of zero to in-school and out-of-school suspensions, to the prospect of becoming a spectacle for their classmates.

Constructing/Maintaining Identity

> Who I think "I" am, then, is a matter that is deeply connected to the language I inherit and, in particular, to the messages I receive about who "I" am or should be, from the others with whom I identify around me. (Piper, 1997, p. 61)

The preceding descriptions make it clear that the social regime of the body constructs specific messages about who students are or should be. The girls prioritized these messages in their lives at school. The power of peers to affix labels that determine social acceptability (Currie, 1999) demonstrates the poststructuralist conception of identity as relational and socially constructed (Miron & Lauria, 1995). As such, the regime of the social body, with its particular discourses, techniques and practices, is a key factor in the ways the subjectivities of individual students are constituted. Many of the participants seemed to experience what Davies (1993) calls the central tension of childhood as the simultaneous struggle to be seamlessly meshed in the social fabric and to know and to signal oneself as a being with specificity. This tension between the desire to be an individual and the push to be the same is expressed by Alicia:

> Individuality is something that I really value. I see myself as an individual. Now, I'm not really concerned about what other people think, but I found that out the hard way. I had an identity crisis. It was hell. I

just didn't know who to be. I didn't know how to act, I didn't know what to say and I didn't know what people would think. The peer thing was pretty bad—nobody liked me, everybody had something against me, and I was so self-conscious. Almost every night I would go home crying because somebody would make fun of me all day. And I always cared what they thought because they were cool. This year I don't really care but it's hard to maintain an identity when the push is to be alike. (06/04/98)

According to another participant, individuality and popularity are directly related:

How much of an individual you can be depends on what group you're in. I think the more popular you are, the easier it is to be an individual because you're already accepted at what you are—you're cool. If you're cool you can wear a loud Hawaiian shirt and no one will say anything. (Angela: 12/03/98)

A certain amount of risk is involved in not conforming to the meanings carried in the agreed-upon social groups at the school. Refusing to be positioned as a Druggie or a Pathetic Wannabe invites the scorn and ridicule of the Popular group. According to Taylor, Gilligan and Sullivan (1995), many students may choose to appear to conform to the standards in order to avoid the risk associated with maintaining an individual voice. August explains why she often remains quiet: "I keep my mouth shut so I don't get the shit kicked out of me. I've been beaten up before, so I've learned the hard way to keep my mouth shut" (06/18/98). But blending in does not necessarily guarantee peer acceptance. Angela speaks disparagingly about the girls she calls "wind-up dolls": "Then there are the girls who do everything they're supposed to. They're pretty, quiet, agreeable, popular and passive. But they're brainless, they have no personality" (03/24/99).

The games of truth in the social regime of the body are complex, brutal, and often contradictory. Even when they deliberately chose not to play the games created by the group, and to contest the meanings assigned to their lives by their peers, the girls were still very much affected by the categories and the techniques and practices of the regime. For some of the participants, the social regime of the body is what made school unbearable.

Cultural Regime of the Body

> Creekwood girls are obsessive about their appearance. Nobody likes how they look. The perfect girl would be skinny and have narrow shoulders, small waist, long legs, big chest, small ears, small nose, straight white teeth, interesting eyes, oval face, no zits, scars, blemishes or facial hair, no freckles. And she would be perfectly proportioned. Even the perfect body doesn't make you happy, but if I were thinner, I'd have it all. (Angela: 05/22/98)

According to Sault (1994) people experience and understand their bodies in accordance with a cultural ideal. In our culture, the outer body of surfaces and appearance is prioritized (Kirk, 1993). Culture's grip on the body (Bordo, 1993) manifests itself in several ways on the bodies of adolescent girls, in their desire to look and be perfect. The contemporary imperative for a perfect body is a social and cultural phenomenon, says Brumberg (1997), that many girls have internalized: "Girls today make the body into an all-consuming project in ways young women of the past did not" (p. xvii). As girls attempt to fit themselves into a singular standard of feminine adolescence (Finders, 1997), their aspirations for perfection extend beyond their bodies. Being perfect, then, includes acceptance of what it means to be a girl. By the age of 10, according to Debold (1995), middle-class girls have combined all of these messages and expectations into the ideal of the "Perfect Girl" who is pretty, kind, obedient and never has bad thoughts or feelings. Furthermore, these messages of femininity are reinforced by schooling practices (Kelly, 1997). The borders between the cultural regime and the institutional regime are porous.

Cultural representations of femininity and beauty can be found in teen magazines, reinforcing the ideal of the "Perfect Girl" with a perfect body. These magazines narrowly define adolescence as looking good, having boyfriends, and being accepted by peers (Currie, 1999). The images of models in magazines are setting the standard of feminine beauty, according to Bordo (1997):

> Today, teenagers no longer have the luxury of a distinction between what's required of a fashion model and what's required of them; the perfected images have become our dominant reality and have set standards for us all—standards that are increasingly unreal in their demands on us. (p. 116)

Certainly, the girls in this study were avid teen magazine readers, and they appeared to accept magazine images as the dominant reality in their quest for the perfect body:

> In my room, I've got pictures from magazines all over. People that I want to look like, be like. (Angela: 03/28/99)

*   *   *   *

> I want to be a model when I grow up. I want to be just like them—skinny. But I need to be taller. Luckily I'm naturally skinny. And the guys like me because I'm skinny. (Emma: 06/15/98)

*   *   *   *

Images, then, invite comparisons and "they are constant reminders of what we are and might with effort yet become"(Featherstone, 1991, p. 178). Some of the students at the Creekwood site believed in the values carried by magazine images; that is, they worked on their bodies in order to achieve greater popularity. This group of girls was called Magazine Girls: "The Try-Hard Girls are the Magazine Girls. They want to be like the models so they copy their trends. They think that they're the most popular" (Angela: 12/03/98).

Techniques and Practices

According to Allen (1996), culturally encoded understandings are reflected in the development of social practices. Destructive discourses (Davies, 1992) about adolescence and about femininity are present in the school, shaping the techniques and practices by which girls aspire to the ideal of the Perfect Girl with a perfect body. This chapter highlights body talk (the ways that the participants talked about their bodies) and body work (the efforts the girls made to improve their bodies) to demonstrate culture's grip on the bodies of adolescent girls. Many of these practices could be described as practices of the self; that is, these techniques involve a relationship of power that is directed on the self to achieve a specific effect. As Hepburn (1997) notes, "we exert power over ourselves by constructing ourselves in particular ways" (p. 34). Although individual girls in this study chose to do certain things to their bodies, the role of agency must not be over-determined. These practices are not invented by individuals, says Foucault (1987) but are proposed, suggested and imposed by culture, society and social group. As active agents the girls are constructing their own histories, "but, of course, a normalizing discourse is internalized from the larger culture" (Finders, 1997, p. 18). When I asked the girls why they felt such pressure to conform to what they had defined as the popular body image, they maintained that it was not because it was popular; rather, they just liked the image and felt it was "normal" (Focus Group: 06/04/98).

LOSING WEIGHT Nichter and Vuckovic (1994) use the term "body work" to describe directed effort to improve the body in an attempt to achieve perfection. These efforts, or disciplinary practices, are designed to "produce a body which in gesture and appearance is recognizably feminine" (Bartky, 1990, p. 65). These practices include those that produce a body of a certain size and configuration, such as dieting and exercising; those that bring forth a specific repertoire of gestures, postures and movements; and those directed toward the display of the body as an ornamented surface. All the participants engaged in forms of body work, because, as Lynne notes, "Some girls are born with the perfect body, but most have to work at it" (06/08/98).

The appeal of slenderness, says Bordo (1997), is over-determined in our culture, and children in this culture grow up knowing that you can never be thin enough. This sentiment was echoed by one of the girls during a focus group: "As long as I'm not fat then I don't care what I look like. I would feel really upset if I got like really really fat" (06/04/98). As a result of this concern with being slender, the type of body work most prevalent at both sites involved attempts to lose weight, as the following anecdotes illustrate:

> I was obsessed with being thinner. I took diet pills and pills that made me throw up. But then my hair started coming out, I was always tired, and I got this rash all over my arms. I think it was from all those pills. I lost a lot of weight and I got more attention from the guys. (Angela: 03/28/99)

*   *   *   *

I've tried to lose weight in a hurry, but I don't like using a laxative. That was disgusting. After taking them for a while, it's like "Hey, I'm not losing hardly any weight at all, and it's just making me feel disgusting." So I stopped. Then, for a while, I just didn't eat as much as I normally did. I felt fine. Every once in a while my stomach would growl and I'm just like, "I'm not hungry." I'm not really embarrassed about my size, just sort of. I'm bigger and taller than all the people in the popular group. That's bad. It makes me feel weird. (Raye: 11/25/98)

*　　*　　*　　*

I've dieted in ways that aren't very healthy. Like not eating for a while so that you can wear a certain pair of pants again. (Sheresa: 06/08/98)

*　　*　　*　　*

Sometimes it's okay to make yourself throw up after eating. I do it when I feel that I ate too much. You eat lunch and then throw up to lose weight. Some people do it and they don't even need to! (Angela: 06/16/98)

*　　*　　*　　*

In addition to speaking to the ways that weight loss has become a normalized practice among adolescent girls, these anecdotes suggest a strong relationship between appearance and popularity. Not only is thinness an important criterion for belonging to the Popular group, it is also seen as an important factor in attracting boys ("I got more attention from the guys" and "the guys like me because I'm skinny"). Jaffee and Lutter (1995) found a similar relationship in their study. For many of their participants, being attractive to boys seemed to be linked to becoming thin and beautiful. And attracting boys makes you even more popular, according to Brenda (11/25/98). In this way, the social and cultural regimes of the body are mutually reinforcing: "the imperative to maintain a thin, toned body is not merely a matter of aesthetics. Bound into the image are expectations and hopes for acceptance—thin females are popular, desirable, and successful"(Nichter & Vuckovic, 1994, p. 126). However, this is not to say that the bodies of all thin females are read in a positive light. For example, one of the girls in the Loser group at Creekwood was slender, and this was used as an excuse to exclude her: "She's so thin it's gross. It's disgusting. You don't want to be around her, it's like ewwwwww"(Brenda: 11/25/98).

"CHEWING OUT OUR BODIES" Nichter & Vuckovic (1994) define girl talk as discussion among friends that functions as a mechanism of social control by encouraging girls to measure themselves against the standards set by the group. Body talk is a form of girl talk that specifically involves girls measuring themselves against standards set by magazines and by friendship groups. In the following example, Angela describes a body talk practice that she calls "chewing out our bodies":

> I get together with my friends and we chew out our bodies. You make a whole bunch of popcorn and you get a whole bunch of candy and you drink pop and watch TV and feel really bad about yourself. Then you stand in front of the mirror and you say, "I hate this about my body and I hate that about my body." And your friends act like "Oh no, you're so pretty. Don't even worry about it." You say those things because you think about those things all the time. "Oh, I'm so fat. I hate it so much." And you say it to your friends and you feel so much better because then they know you're self-conscious about it and they won't say anything about it on purpose. (Angela: 05/22/98)

Body talk is not confined to girl talk, though. The girls in this study reported that their male classmates often made comments about their bodies: "They say I'm fat, even though I know I'm not. Like I'm not slim or anything, but I'm not seriously overweight" (Raye: 06/04/98). Comments were also of a sexual nature (e.g., skanky-ass whore), leading to what Watkinson (1997) describes as a learning environment poisoned by sexual harassment. Rarely did teachers intervene in this kind of talk, similar to the findings of the AAUW Report (1992):

> When boys line up to "rate" girls as they enter a room, when boys treat girls so badly they are reluctant to enroll in courses where they may be the only female, when boys feel it is fun to embarrass girls to the point of tears, it is not a joke. Yet these types of behaviors are often viewed by school personnel as harmless instances of "boys being boys." (p. 73)

Tacit acceptance of this kind of talk perpetuates the notion that it is normal and that boys will be boys. Even when incidents such as these are not viewed as entirely harmless, school personnel may be averting their gazes (pretending not to notice) in order to avoid dealing with issues of gender. Not addressing these issues, though, means that girls will unquestioningly accept these discourses as well: "The guys are critical of our bodies. You've got to laugh it off. Get something back at them" (Angela: 05/22/98).

"I'm Fat"

The girls in this study engaged in body work and body talk in their pursuit of the perfect body. The participants from both sites, when asked to describe the perfect body, were unanimous about the standard of female beauty, a standard conveyed to them, in part, through the images found in teen magazines. These girls reported great unhappiness with their own bodies, replicating the findings of other studies. The pressure to conform to an ideal shape can be a source of acute anxiety because "there are genetic limits to the kind of body we are capable of achieving" (Kirk, 1993, p. 12). Brenda acknowledges that she is critical of her body and that she works hard trying to bring her body into line with the ideal of the perfect body: "I know I'm hard on myself. I do it to myself. I know what I am and what I'd like to be" (05/22/98).

But as they try to attain the impossible, the perfected images that are their dominant reality (Bordo, 1997), they also begin to judge themselves through other's eyes and to question their worth (Debold, 1995). Bright, capable, healthy girls make statements such as this: "I'm fat. I wish that I could say I'm thin enough or pretty enough. I don't like how I look. I know I'm clumsy and not that smart" (Angela: 05/22/98). The negative thinking and talking about the body expressed by Angela and the other girls likely do little to alleviate the overall feelings of anxiety about their bodies. Body talk and body work have a normalizing function; that is, these techniques and practices impose homogeneity as they compare, hierarchize and exclude (Foucault, 1975). In the cultural regime of the body, the disciplinary gaze becomes interiorized:

Preoccupation with fat, diet, and slenderness are not abnormal. Indeed, such preoccupation may function as one of the most powerful normalizing mechanisms of our century, insuring the production of self-monitoring and self-disciplining "docile bodies" sensitive to any departure from social norms and habituated to self-improvement and self-transformation in the service of those norms. (Bordo, 1993, p. 186)

Competing Regimes of Truth

Historically, psychiatrists and psychologists have marked adolescence as a particularly difficult time in women's development (Gilligan, 1991). Young women "exhibit low self-esteem, are afraid for their safety, have to deal with unwanted attention, and are expected to play outdated roles. In Canada today, young females continue to feel significantly inferior to young males when it comes to general competence" (Bibby and Posterski, 1992, p. 21). Pipher (1994) agrees that adolescence is a difficult time for females:

Something dramatic happens to girls in early adolescence. Just as planes and ships disappear mysteriously into the Bermuda Triangle, so do the selves of adolescent girls go down in droves. They crash and burn in a social and development Bermuda Triangle. In early adolescence, studies show that girls' IQ scores drop and their math and science scores plummet. They lose their resiliency and optimism and become less curious and inclined to take risks. They lose their assertive, energetic and "tomboyish" personalities and become more deferential, self-critical and depressed. They report great unhappiness with their own bodies. (p. 21)

The voices and the actions of the girls in this study attest to the fact that adolescence is a difficult time for females. At school, girls inhabit a space where multiple regimes of truth flourish, and this is indeed a difficult space within which to live. Many of the girls echoed the sentiment expressed by Angela: "In a million ways it's just easier not to go to school."

Part of the difficulty arises from the competing meanings within the regimes of the body and across the regimes. The docile body of the institutional regime is not the kind of body that the girls aspire to within the social and cultural regimes of the body. And even within the social and cultural regimes, the meanings of the body are not stable. The next chapter, chapter 7, will illustrate the simultaneous operation of the multiple and competing regimes of the body. Physical education classes, in particular, are locations where the girls seemed to experience the tensions of competing regimes.

seven

Schooling the Body in Physical Education

THE GIRLS IN THIS STUDY REPEATEDLY EXPRESSED THEIR DISLIKE for physical education and discussed strategies they developed for avoiding physical education. In this chapter, resistance to physical education is discussed as a response to: 1) the official curriculum and instruction of physical education, 2) intolerable peer relations, and/or, 3) dominant cultural messages about femininity. Physical education classes, in particular, seem to be sites where the regimes of the body identified in chapter 6 are integrated. The conclusion of this chapter demonstrates how the institutional, cultural and social regimes of the body that are integrated within physical education classes create a site of struggle for adolescent girls. This struggle is particularly concerned with identity: regimes of the body frame certain modes of thinking and being, shaping and limiting the range of identities made available.

* * * *

We skip Phys. Ed. because it's totally embarrassing. We started skipping it the second day of school this year. We don't like people staring.

Everybody watches you and makes comments, even the teacher. Sometimes the teacher makes you go up in front of the whole class and do a
demonstration. And the whole class comments when you walk back to
your place. They insult you and say mean stuff. The boys—they have
a big mouth. Like they started commenting on our chests in grade six.
(Rebecca and Diane: 12/10/98)

*   *   *   *

Phys. Ed., I don't like, especially demonstrations in front of the whole
class and there's a whole bunch of eyes staring at you. I didn't mind in
grade four, but now, it's like, "Oh God, help me" and I turn all red. I'd
rather have girls-only P.E. classes because then you don't have men looking at you. They're stupid and they don't understand. Like they don't
know the emotional pain they cause when they call you bad names. Of
course they do it when the teacher isn't listening. Some of the boys are
nice but most of them are a pain in the butt. (Lynn: 06/18/98)

*   *   *   *

I don't like P.E. Everyone's always watching. It makes you really self-conscious. You're always being evaluated by your teachers and your peers.
You get made fun of in P.E. because you look stupid. When I don't have
to take P.E. anymore, I'm not going to. (Angela: 12/03/98)

*   *   *   *

According to Kirk (1993) physical education has been a key site in
which the body is schooled. Not only is the body schooled through
the use of institutional power, as many theorists have discussed, the
body is also schooled culturally and socially within physical education classes. Schools are located within the machinery of cultural
and social regulation (Gore, 1993). Institutional, cultural and social regimes of the body are integrated at the site of the school, and
the school integrates specific techniques and practices and dominant
discourses of the regimes. Using the example of physical education
class, the discourses and practices from the various regimes of the
body are shown to provide the participants with what Davies (1993)
calls multiple layers of contradictory meaning.

"I Hate Phys. Ed."

Every girl in this study spoke at length about her negative feelings toward physical education classes. It would be easy to assume that the girls simply disliked physical activity, hence their dislike of physical education class. Jaffee and Manzer (1992) maintained that in their study 100% of the girls reported enjoying physical activity, but that they also cited serious obstacles to their participation in physical education: "These obstacles included unfair treatment by the boys they were playing with, (and) the assumption that they were not good players" (p. 23). Similarly, Angela reported that she enjoyed playing ringette and soccer outside of school, Rebecca and Diane liked walking, and August enjoyed skateboarding. Clearly, there is something amiss when physically active girls refuse to participate in physical education classes. As the examples at the beginning of the chapter illustrate, the causes for negative feelings about physical education are varied, but they are not necessarily linked to negative perceptions of physical activity. Rather, these negative feelings can be traced to competing modes of thinking and being that are framed not only by the institutional regime of the body but also by the social and cultural regimes.

These contradictory meanings result in a school culture that is a "complex venue within which to develop a sense of self" (Currie, 1999, p. 243). Currie uses the terms "doing" and "undoing" of the subject to capture processes of subjectivity. Doing refers to those processes that facilitate girls' sense of individuality in school, while undoing refers to processes "such as worrying about looks and being labeled by others, which unsettle girls' sense of Self and worth as social beings" (Currie, 1999, p. 209). In physical education classes, the selves of girls are both "done" and "undone," as described by Currie, as they are constituted in the institutional, cultural and social regimes of the body. In the following section of the chapter, institutional, cultural, and social barriers to participation in physical education are described.

Physical Education Curriculum

As the anecdotes at the beginning of the chapter illustrate, there seem to be multiple causes for negative feelings about physical education. The official curriculum of physical education, however, appears to be a major influence in the construction of resistance. In other words, negative perceptions regarding physical education are associated with the activities and their instruction. For example, Diane maintained that she liked physical activity, but not the physical activities within physical education class:

> I don't like P.E. It's not the physical things, it's just the things we do are stupid. Running around the gym 10,000 times. Doing push-ups in a certain way, and he makes us go chin down. We can't even do those kind of push-ups, they're the boy's kind, and he makes us do them anyway. He makes us do 20 of them and we can't even do one. (05/19/98)

These kinds of activities may lead to student resistance, as students refuse to participate in "stupid" activities. In the next example, Angela describes how a specific activity leads to skipping physical education classes:

> I can't do the endurance run. I tried but I threw up. I could only do 8 laps out of 12. Now the teacher is trying to make me do it again. I know I'll just fail it again. I won't go to PE until they're finished fitness testing. (06/16/99)

For both Diane and Angela, resistance to physical education is structured by specific activities. These kinds of activities are part of a multiactivity skills and sports curriculum that is based on a European, male, middle-class, sporting model (Ennis, 1995). It is a curriculum where male-defined standards of power and strength predominate (Vertinsky, 1992). This form of activity is called exercise, the techniques by which one imposes on the body tasks that are repetitive (Foucault, 1975). According to Foucault (1975), exercise has a long history; "it is to be found in military, religious and university practices" (p. 161). This kind of exercise, conjuring up images of drill sergeants leading their soldiers in tightly controlled forms of calisthenics, continues to be practiced in schools. Running around the gym 10,000 times and regimented drills for push-ups are examples of Foucault's definition of exercise. Physical education continues to be narrowly defined by many physical education teachers as a combination of exercise and traditional sports (basketball, volleyball, soccer) that are highly competitive and in which boys take control in such a way as to limit girls' participation (Jaffee & Manzer, 1992). These exercises and traditional sports are the activities in which many girls choose not to participate. In this way, the official curriculum in physical education structured obstacles to participation in physical education for the girls in this study.

"Everyone's Always Watching"

Another barrier to participation is the sense of being under surveillance. At school, girls are scrutinized by their teachers, their peers (both boys and girls) and themselves. These gazes are integrated at the site of the school, leading to conditions that Foucault (1975) describes by using Bentham's idea of the Panopticon, in which "inspections functions ceaselessly. The gaze is alert everywhere" (p. 195). At school, forms of institutional, cultural and social surveillance occur, and one cannot escape from the network of simultaneous gazes: "Everyone's always watching," said Angela (12/03/98). These gazes can have both an "undoing" and a "doing" effect on the selves of girls. The notion of simultaneous gazes that "undo" is illustrated in physical education classes by the practice of demonstrations—those times when an individual is selected by the teacher to demonstrate her competence in a particular skill. The teacher's gaze is an evaluative gaze; that is, the teacher watches the student perform the skill, often noting on a clipboard her level of competence. At the same time, the student is being scrutinized by her peer group. When the student finishes her demonstration and returns to her place, she must be mindful of the unwanted comments about her body made by her male classmates. These comments are reflective of the cultural regime, where this form of body talk is tolerated under the rubric of "boys will be boys." Physical education, with its focus on the body, seems to invite comments about the body, such as the following:

> I've been made fun of in gym. Because I look funny when I run, I've heard. I'm really self-conscious about my legs. They flop all over. (Brenda: 11/25/98)

*   *   *   *

Okay, you're either too flat or you're too big. And they'll make fun of you either way. Like in gym one guy said I'm flat. And then another one says I'm huge. I don't think you can be both! (Raye: 06/04/98)

*   *   *   *

And of course, before, during, and after the demonstration, the student is conscious of her own body—how she is walking, how she is performing ("Are my legs flopping?", "Do I look funny?"). The gaze is turned inward as the girls attempt to monitor the outward appearance of their bodies. Based on the participants' discussions of these demonstrations, it seems that this practice, in every instance, unsettles the girls' sense of self. Demonstrations in physical education are a process of "undoing" the self. Resistance can emerge as students evaluate one another's bodies and performances in physical education.

Spectacle and Display

Although the girls in this study were sensitive to the gazes of others, they also, at times, welcomed the opportunity to display their bodies: "Phys. Ed. is a chance to show off for anybody of the opposite sex. Girls like to show off if there's a guy that they like or they think is cute or whatever" (Raye: 11/25/98). This is an example of the manifestation in physical education of the culturally acceptable practice of displaying the body (Featherstone, 1991).

One way to show off and to attract the attention of boys is through dress, a practice described by Rebecca as "flogging yourself" over guys:

The Snob Squad—they dress with all the tight clothes to show off their bodies. And they want the guys, that's the whole point. That's what they do it for—the guys. So the girls just do that to make the guys want to like them because that's the whole point. They want the guys to notice them and think that they're cool. (12/10/98)

At the same time, though, wearing the "wrong" clothes may invite the wrong kind of attention: "You don't wear shirts that the guys can look down into because then you are a slut" (Focus Group: 06/04/98). There is a delicate balance between attracting boys and being labeled a slut. Girls must also strike a balance regarding the amount of attention they receive from the boys, because too much or too little attention is not desirable: "If every single guy likes you, then all the girls hate you" (Focus Group: 06/04/98).

The regimes of the body regulate the body's dress in various ways. The social regime disciplines the appearance of the body by prescribing acceptable and unacceptable dress (tight shirts are allowed, low necklines are not allowed). These prescriptions are reinforced by the cultural regime, wherein it is acceptable to display the body in order to attract the attention of the opposite sex: "You're always trying to dress up for the guys" (Focus Group: 06/04/98). The institutional regime also regulates the body's dress. The dress code, as noted in chapter 6, prohibits displaying shoulders and belly buttons. However, it does not prohibit tight clothing or low necklines. Even though shoulders and belly buttons are concealed, other parts of the body may be revealed. Girls can attract the attention of the boys while still complying with the dress code. Once again, they are "fooling" the institution.

The dress of the body is more tightly controlled in physical education. At both school sites, students were expected to change into shorts and tee shirts. In fact, changing for physical education was a rule and thus became a disciplinary issue. The participants reported that some girls welcomed the opportunity to show off their bodies by wearing short shorts and tight tee shirts. Other girls, however, refused to change for physical education (Focus Group: 06/04/98). Six of the participants (Alicia, Angela, Raye, Diane, Rebecca and August) insisted on wearing loose and baggy clothing. These students seemed to resist the practice of displaying their bodies by refusing to change into prescribed clothing yet their actions were most often interpreted by their teachers as "defiance." And Brenda, who was very self-conscious about her floppy "white" legs, refused to wear shorts unless she had been sun tanning. "With a tan," she said, "I look healthier and a little sexier, too" (06/04/98).

The distinction between spectacle and display is a subtle one. The girls wanted to attract the attention of the boys by displaying their bodies, yet they did not want to become spectacles, or sluts, because of the way they dressed. They seemed to think it was possible to control their image through their dress and were confused when their intended message (attractiveness) was misinterpreted by the boys as invitations for sexual advances. In some cases, then, display of the body can be seen as a process of "doing" the self because it appears to facilitate a girl's sense of self as being attractive to the opposite sex. Becoming a spectacle, on the other hand, is a process of "undoing" the self, especially when a girl's body is misread and she is labeled by her peers as a slut.

Looking Good/Being Popular: The Cultural and the Social

According to Currie (1999), school culture reinforces the definitions of femininity and ways of being female that are offered by teen magazines. These discourses from society at large are embedded in the overt curriculum of physical education, and most students comply with traditional feminine and masculine roles in the ways they participate in physical education (Chepaytor-Thomson & Ennis, 1997). In the next anecdote, Raye demonstrates how she has internalized the dominant cultural messages of femininity. She also links physical activity to looking good, a feat accomplished only by the popular girls. The cultural regime (looking good) and the social regime (being popular) are conjoined in physical education and mutually reinforce their respective messages:

> Girls, they're expected to be graceful, always in control, be able to do basically everything. Even if a girl gets a red face from running too much, they're expected to be calm and be able to look good all the time. But if you have a red sweaty face, the guys are like, "Ooh, yuck! What have you been doing?" Some girls try hard in phys. ed. I think it's weird. But the popular girls seem to look good all the time. They can be running for an hour, and their faces aren't red. They might be breathing hard, but they look perfectly fine. I don't really like sweating at all. (11/04/98)

In this example, the cultural definition of femininity (girls don't sweat) seems to take precedence over attempts to attain the perfect body. In an earlier interview, Raye insisted that she needed to work out more in order to lose weight. To engage in body work, working out to lose weight and to tone muscles, without sweating, might be a difficult task for Raye.

The physical education teacher may also reinforce cultural definitions of femininity through his teaching practices. Angela describes how the practice of forming teams differentiates between girls and boys:

> We have gym with a grade seven class. This year Mr. Day makes teams with the grade seven girls, the weakest, and the grade eight boys, the strongest. They play against the grade seven boys and the grade eight girls, they're in the middle. He's trying to even out the teams. The message is that the boys are best and the gym teacher thinks they're best. (12/03/98)

The message that girls are second-class citizens in the physical education classroom (Nilges, 1998) has been clearly conveyed to Angela. When students perceive sex-biased standards favoring males in physical education class (AAUW Report, 1992) they may choose to resist participating.

Rebecca also links the cultural regime to the social regime, but in this instance she describes an incident that contradicts the cultural definition of femininity. Here, meanness is directed towards boys by the girls:

> The Snob Squad even wants to be perfect in gym. Like their perfectness extends everywhere in the school. They have to be the focus of everything. They made a guy cry in gym one time. That's one of the things they like to do. It makes them feel like they actually accomplished something. (02/17/99)

In this instance, an exclusionary practice of the social regime outweighed one of the tenets of the cultural definition of femininity, contradicting a common gendered discourse of "girls are nice and boys are tough" (Thorne, 1993, p. 105).

A Site of Struggle

> This theme of struggle only really becomes operative if one establishes concretely—in each particular case—who is engaged in struggle, what the struggle is about, and how, where, by what means and according to what rationality it evolves. (Foucault, 1982a, p. 164)

Physical education, in addition to many other places in the school, seemed to be a site of struggle for the participants in this study.

The students repeatedly expressed their dislike for physical education and developed many strategies for avoiding physical education including skipping class, disappearing into the change room after attendance had been taken, refusing to change into gym clothes, and not participating:

> I avoid the comments by not doing all the stuff that the teacher tells us to. Because if you don't do the skills, then the others can't comment. So you just kind of wait things out and hope he doesn't notice. One time we were playing soccer and I didn't want to play. He made me go in the field for defense and I just stood there. So he kicked the ball right to me, and I kicked it right out of the field on purpose. That was the end of that. (Diane: 05/19/98)

"What is the struggle about?" Foucault asks. Specifically, the struggle in physical education can be viewed as a struggle for identity. The institutional, cultural and social regimes of the body that are integrated within physical education classes frame certain modes of thinking and being, shaping and limiting the range of identities for adolescent girls. Often, the participants refused the subject positions offered by these regimes. Foucault (1982a) calls this the struggle against the submission of subjectivity, noting that "Maybe the target nowadays is not to discover what we are, but to refuse who we are" (p. 216).

In the institutional regime, the struggle can be characterized as refusal to accept the identity being assigned by the school (Erickson, 1987). A "good student" refers to someone who is conscientious, compliant, and modest (Harper, 1997), someone whom Angela would call a "wind-up doll." The production of docile bodies and ordered multiplicities of wind-up dolls (the institutional definition of student lives) is resisted by some students. As adolescents move beyond the elementary school, they are more inclined to question the role adults have assigned (Ennis, 1995).

In physical education, the techniques and practices of the institutional regime are largely concerned with regulating the movements of the body:

The control of groups of children on playing fields and in gymnasiums also continues to be an important skill in the repertoires of physical educators. And physical education lessons are still paradigm cases of attempts to organize time and space on and around pupils' bodies. (Kirk, 1993, p. 51)

The activities and games organized on the bodies of the students (the physical education curriculum) defined the girls in particular ways. They received messages about being weak, clumsy and inept. Some of the instances of resistance to physical education ("He tries to make me participate. But I won't") were certainly attempts to resist the notion of having one's body controlled and defined in particular ways by the institutional authority of the teacher.

In the social regime, a number of struggles concerning identity are apparent. According to Alicia's narrative, the struggle to be an individual when the push is to be the same was a source of tension. Asserting the right to be different was difficult for both Alicia and Diane. For other students, like Raye, who desperately wanted to be accepted by the Popular group, the struggle concerns the attempt to bring oneself more into line with the group's definition of what is acceptable. Raye decided to change her look and her personality in order to be accepted. Angela's struggle involved her attempts to remain popular; she was very conscious of the gazes of her peers. The girls at both sites spoke of the difficulty of attracting the attention of boys without being identified as a slut by their peers. However, attracting the wrong kind of attention, or too much attention, caused problems with their friendship groups. The complexity of social relationships between and across friendship groups seemed to be intensified in physical education.

The struggle inherent in the cultural regime of the body did not involve resistance to the ideal of the perfect body. Rather, this struggle was concerned with attaining the perfect body. The participants were actively involved in the "perpetual quest of the elusive yet ruthlessly normalizing goal, the 'perfect' body" (Bordo, 1993, p. 248). According to Bartky (1990), identity cannot be kept separate from the appearance of our bodies. Therefore, less-than-perfect bodies impact sense of self. As Raye explains, "I'd like to have a body that makes me feel good about myself" (06/04/98).

Overall, the experience of being an adolescent girl at school, especially in physical education, and the struggles for identity led participants to make comments such as: "It's just so complicated, I just don't want to deal with it anymore" (Rebecca: 02/17/99). In light of the various, and sometimes conflicting, regimes of the body, it is not surprising, as Harper (1997) suggests, that adolescence is often a traumatic time for girls, as they "negotiate themselves through the quagmire of adolescent experience and beyond in an expanded horizon of possibilities" (p. 159).

Who Am I? Who Do I Wish To Be?

Desire is a key component in the struggle for identity in the official and unofficial spaces of the school (in classrooms, the office, corridors, lunch rooms and playgrounds). Harper (1997) argues from the perspective of psychoanalytic theory that desire and identification are keys to the structuring of identity—that is, "who one wishes to be (identification) and who one wishes to have (desire) organize a play of difference and similitude in self-other relations that define or mark boundaries of recognizable identity" (Harper, 1997, p. 142). Desire is not only whom one wishes to have. It is also concerned with the wishes one has for the self. Kelly (1997) locates desire as the shape dreams and identities take in the social, and she names the body "as the site on which meanings of identity, difference, desire, knowledge, social worth, and possibility are assimilated and contested" (p. 31). Individual desires structured the kinds of self-styling that the girls participated in, and the regimes of the body attempted to structure the desires of the girls in particular ways. Kelly (1997) uses the term mind/ing the body to refer to ways the school attempts to produce particular forms of subjectivity: "The notion of *mind/ing bodies* bespeaks most accurately and succinctly how the intersection of knowledge, power, and desire craft identity as the cultural project of schools" (p. 1).

Harper (1997) suggests renaming resistance as understanding and learning to work with the power of identification and desire. This renaming more fully captures the struggle for identity that much resistance seems to be about: reframing the prevalent themes in the analysis as "wanting" and "not wanting" makes it possible to discover what the participants desire of their own bodies and the bodies of others, and how these desires structure identity and the struggle for identity. These desires are, of course, shaped and constrained by the institutional, cultural and social regimes of the body. They are interconnected and in conflict (Harper, 1997).

The desires of young women, formed in the social, may not be the same desires that schooling practices hope to instill. The desire of the institutional regime is the production of docile bodies and ordered multiplicities. To promote their desire, schools must discipline the desires of their students through particular forms of social control (Kelly, 1997) or the techniques and practices of the institutional regime of the body. Fine (1992) notes that within today's standard sex education curricula and many public school classrooms, we find "the authorized suppression of a discourse of female desire" (p. 76). The attempted regulation of female sexual desire through the sex education curriculum, occurring at the same time as girls are actively constructing boys as objects of their desire, is one example of how the meaning of a particular (sexual) desire is simultaneously interconnected and in conflict.

The body is "the site on which meanings of identity, difference, desire, knowledge, social worth and possibility are assimilated and contested" (Kelly, 1997, p. 31). The desires of (some) adolescent girls in this study included wishing to be pretty, popular, and slender and to attract the attention of boys. All of the girls expressed a desire for belongingness, although to "what" they desired to belong had different meanings. The desire to belong, expressed by Roman (1996) as desires for community, affiliation, recognition and commitment, also "articulates the terms of marginalization and inclusion" (p. 9). Not all girls share the same desires or define a common desire (belonging) in the same way. Some of the participants in this study did not share the dominant desires. Their desires, to be independent, to look, act and think differently than the majority, were also assimilated/contested on their bodies, and articulated their marginalization from the dominant social groups at school. Schools are complicit in structuring, and sometimes even promoting, all of these desires. At the site of the school, the dominant desires of the regimes of the body are both interconnected and in conflict.

Summary

Competing regimes of the body make and mold the bodies of adolescent girls in particular ways, shaping and limiting the range of subject positions for these young women. The discourses integrated by, through, and in these regimes are constraining:

> How we live our lives as conscious thinking subjects, and how we give meaning to the material social relations under which we live and which structure our everyday lives, depends on the range of existing discourses, our access to them. (Weedon, 1987, p. 26)

Analysis of the data demonstrated at a very concrete level how the discourses of the regimes of the body structure and give meaning to the lives of the participants. The discourses of adolescence and female adolescence, of "'girls are nice' and 'boys are tough'" (Thorne, 1993, p. 105), of dominant notions of masculinities and femininities, provided the participants with the language categories within which to interpret and describe their lives and their desires. Often, these discourses were very narrow in focus and were considered to be "normal." They reinforced one another within and across particular regimes of the body. For example, as Harper (1997) found, teenage girls believe it normal to be "obsessed" with boys. This message is reinforced in the teen magazines that offer advice on how to "get" a boyfriend, and in the social regime where being popular includes having a boyfriend. Girls constitute boys as objects of their desire and central to their identity as girls (Harper, 1997). Interventions that can "break open the range of identities possible" and create a new horizon of possibilities (Harper, 1997, p. 158) in the face of firmly entrenched categories of living and being will be discussed in the next chapter.

eight

"The Impossible Underbelly of Possibility"

Introduction

THE TITLE FOR THIS CHAPTER COMES FROM KELLY'S (1997) DISCUS-
sion of poststructuralist theory and the ways in which it is attuned
to human struggle. Human struggle from this perspective acknowledges the complexities of systems of meaning in the construction of
self. For the girls in this study, the human struggle included institutional, cultural and social pressures that attempted to constrain their
bodies and their identities in particular ways. At school, the regimes
of the body positioned the girls in particular ways. The institutional
regime, for example, positioned students as docile bodies. In the social regime, peers affixed labels on each other that represented social
competence and the degree of social acceptability. And in the cultural regime, girls' bodies were positioned as inadequate and lacking.
The school represented a place where these co-mingling discourses
produce a social context of complexity and instability, demonstrat-
ing how conflicting subjectivities are produced in/through relationships of power/knowledge. I agree with Kelly (1997) that schools are
implicated in the production of subjectivities, and that this production may well involve human struggle.

Within the context of schooling, adolescents negotiate the difficult terrain of adolescence and engage in the search for a social self, which is the central task of teenagerhood (Currie, 1999). For students, this search can become a struggle as the institutional, cultural and social regimes of the body act to produce bodies and craft identities of specific types. Many times the girls in this study struggled against assuming ready-made identities (e.g., "good student," Loser, Druggie, or Wannabe). Their eruptions of difference as they refused to be positioned by the regimes, however, were more than moves against a particular form of power. For in their resistance to the submission of subjectivity, they tried to actively constitute themselves as other than what was being suggested or imposed by the regimes. In this chapter, an alternative interpretation of resistance is suggested and it is then connected to ideas about curriculum in general, and more specifically, to the curriculum of physical education.

Resistance to Identity

The girls at both school sites in this study expressed similar concerns about their lives at school, and these concerns transcended the difference in their geographical location. Common themes of disengagement from school, the absence of caring relationships, the appearance of the body, and the harshness of the social relations between students are themes that might be identified by other girls within Western culture. Specific to the girls in this study, though, was a seemingly heightened struggle for identity, reflective of what Donald (cited in Ellsworth, 1997) describes as resistance to identity:

> This resistance is tied to an often unconscious feeling that we are—we must be—more than the selves that our cultures, our schools, our government, our families, our social norms and expectations are offering us or demand us to be. (p. 44)

The girls seemed sensitive to the tension between the singular subject positions offered or demanded by the regimes and their own experiences. In re-theorizing their resistance, it might more aptly be called resistance to identity. They recognized, at some level, that

self is multiple and contingent in that it is always positioned in relation to history, desires and circumstances (Britzman, 1991). The
girls were aware that they wore many masks as they moved from one
context to another (Piper, 1997). When I asked Angela, for example,
to describe herself, she responded that it depended on who she was
with and what she was doing. In fact, she used a mask metaphor to
describe her variety of selves (12/12/98). Angela seemed to recognize
that identities can never be contained in any one moment or place, as
Currie (1999) says. She was not simply a "good girl" or a "good student" or a "good daughter," the subject positions demanded of her by
her culture, her school and her parents. The struggle for identity for
Angela and for the other girls involved refusing singular and unified
subject positions. It was a struggle, often taking many forms, against
the submission of subjectivity (Foucault, 1982a).

The girls accepted, desired, created, challenged and refused subject positions suggested or imposed by the regimes of truth in the
school. They questioned the roles that adults and peers assigned.
There is no one single story of resistance, and although their individual responses to the regimes were not universal, they demonstrated a critical stance to the constraining range of identities offered.

The participants, then, constituted themselves actively, as Foucault (1987) maintains, and they wanted to believe that the choices
they made were their own (Bordo, 1997). Yet their choices, and the
practices of the self in which they engaged, were located within regimes of the body at the site of the school. This is the relationship
between the subject and games of truth: the subject is constituted
through practices which are games of truth (Foucault, 1987). The
girls were neither totally constrained nor totally free. For example,
they organized their thinking about themselves around their bodies rather than questioning the cultural constructs that encouraged
them to believe that their bodies were defective, lacking, and inadequate. The practices of the self that constituted their bodies in
particular ways were masked, as Bordo (1997) says, by the rhetoric
of agency.

According to Piper (1997), the modernist program in schooling
is one that promotes the development of a stable, singular and unified self. The cultural and social regimes of the body also offered
narrowly defined subject positions. The girls in this study seemed to

reject this notion of the self, as it did not fit with their experiences. The alternative interpretation of resistance presented here, based on the experiences of the girls in this study, is one that suggests that resistance to schooling might more aptly be called resistance to identity. The challenge for educators adopting this perspective is to consider ways that curriculum might begin to recognize resistance as resistance to identity. The next section of the chapter provides an initial discussion of how curriculum can address students in ways that recognize identity as a matrix of possible subject positions.

Curricula of the Regimes of the Body

The cultural project of schools is to produce bodies and craft identities of specific types (Kelly, 1997). As seen in chapter 6, the various regimes of the body construct identities of particular types, and yet they are interrelated at the site of the school. This cultural project might be one element of what is commonly called the hidden curriculum in schools: those unintended and un-noticed learnings taught implicitly by the school experience (McLaren, 2003). This notion of curriculum, though, does not adequately describe how curriculum itself produces subjectivities. On the other hand, Kelly's (1997) counter-notion of curriculum describes the relationship between curriculum and subjectivity:

> Through the institutional base of schools, curriculum serves as the planned means by which some discourses are legitimated and others marginalized or silenced. Such curriculum positions teachers and students in particular (and regulatory) ways in relation to specified forms of knowledge, through both their absence and presence, and to specific notions of knowledge-production. As such, curriculum is itself a process and practice active in the production of subjectivities, of knowing subjects—schooled subjects—whose engagement with curriculum is relational, that is, based on relations of power into which subjects are (re)positioned differently and inequitably. (p. 18)

Typically, students are on the receiving end of the learning experience within a monolithic curriculum: "it is as if the histories, experience, and communities that shape their identities and sense of place are irrelevant to what is taught and how it is taught" (Giroux,

1994, p. 42). By virtue of their grade level, students are assumed to have similar, if not identical, needs. This is a curriculum that positions students as if they do in fact have fixed and unified subject positions. In the institutional regime, this is indeed one of the ways that schooled subjects (docile bodies) are produced. Kelly's (1997) counter-notion of curriculum shows how the curriculum of the institutional regime is a legitimate discourse at school: curriculum (as a practice of power) produces subjectivities of schooled subjects. Yet the practices, techniques and discourses of the cultural and social regimes might also be termed curriculum. They, too, produce subjectivities of particular types and position students in particular ways. Their curricula are the knowledges that describe the reality produced by the regimes; they are the "set of ideas adequate to the mechanisms of power" (Feher, 1987, p. 161). The institutional base of school includes not only the official and mandated curriculum, it includes cultural and social curriculums and integrates their practices. These curricula are the vehicles by which educational institutions and practices address their students and teachers (Ellsworth, 1997).

Ellsworth (1997) maintains that it is possible to address students in ways that do not require them to assume fixed, singular, unified positions within power and social relations. Address, as noted in chapter 6, describes the ways we take up a position within knowledge, power, and desire in relation to others and assign to them a position in relation to ourselves and to a context. Modes of address set in motion the positions from which they can be met and responded to, but according to Ellsworth there is never an exact fit between address and response. Predicting how students may respond is difficult. For example, the formal curriculum sets in motion responses from the students, but these are rarely the anticipated responses. This lack of fit is what Ellsworth calls the space of difference between address and response. The curricula of the institutional, cultural and social regimes include such spaces of difference. Within these spaces of difference between address and response, the girls in this study seemed to sense, as Donald (1991, cited in Ellsworth, 1997) describes, that they must be more than the selves demanded or offered by the regimes of the body. When curricula do work with students, perhaps it is because of the "who" they are offering students to imagine themselves as being and enacting (Ellsworth, 1997). In the next section, I begin to articulate possibilities within curriculum that may expand the range of subject positions for adolescent girls by addressing them in ways that recognize their multiplicity of selves and that offer girls a "who" that they can imagine themselves being and enacting.

Constituting a New Politics of Truth

Because pedagogy implies both instructional practices and social visions (Gore, 1993), my suggestions are inclusive of both of these realms. "New" games of truth, for living with girls in middle schools in general and in physical education in particular are imagined. Constituting new games, or what Foucault (1980) calls new politics of truth, involves changing the way truth is produced: "The problem is not changing people's consciousness—or what's in their heads—but the political, economic, institutional regime of the production of truth" (p. 133). The possibility always exists, says Foucault (1987), in any regime of truth, to discover something else, to change the rules and sometimes even the totality of the game of truth. Interventions are needed in order to identify spaces for rupture or dislocate particular truths produced by the regimes of the body, because these truths limit the range of identities possible for adolescent girls. They constitute themselves through these games of truth as they fit themselves out with particular truths, or with what I am now calling the regimes' curricula.

The new politics of truth must be constituted within what Gore (1993) calls the irreducible and ineluctable aspects of pedagogy (its location within the machinery of social/cultural regulation and the continuing importance of the teacher in the machinery of moral supervision). For these reasons, it might seem hopeless to imagine a new politics of truth, and, in fact, it is, if one focuses on imagining a new and better institution: "If you wish to replace an official institution by another institution that fulfills the same function—better and differently—then you are already being absorbed by the dominant structure" (Foucault, 1977, p. 232). Rather than making universal suggestions for intervention, ones that would result in "better" schools, I make specific suggestions for my own practice and research, because as Gore (1993) notes, there is always something to be done at the local level. Working at a local level with issues of one's own practice and research is to adopt the role of what Foucault (1980) calls the "specific intellectual," scholars working "within specific sectors, at the precise points where their own conditions of life or work situate them" (p. 126). Even while I consider possible interventions at a local level, I am reminded of Foucault's (1982b) warning that everything is dangerous and of Gore's (1993) cautionary note that no practices or discourses are inherently liberating or oppressive and that our most libratory intentions have no guaranteed effects. Primarily, my suggestions involve reconstituting the teacher-student relationship by engaging in a form of moral inquiry and incorporating into physical education suggestions presented by the girls in this study.

Moral Inquiry

Van Manen (1990) says that we must act responsibly and responsively in our relations with youth. Acting responsibly and responsively with students entails the general moral guideline of protecting the vulnerable (Walker, 1998). It was difficult for me to imagine constituting a new politics of truth from within the discourses of the regimes of truth because Foucault's notion of morals does not seem to take into account the relationships we ought to have with others. Foucault (1982a) defines two aspects of the concept of morals: the moral codes that are imposed upon people, and secondly, the kind of relationship you ought to have with yourself as you constitute yourself as a moral subject (p. 238). The concept of moral imagination, as described by Mason (1999), seems not to have a place within the work of Foucault:

> [The key] is the cultivation of the ability to pay caring attention to the experience that someone is undergoing at a particular time, to the "experience in the room." This is not always an easy thing to do. Nor is it something for which there are protocols. There is no algorithm, no recipe, no rule for attending to the right things at the right time. (p. K6)

While our moral imaginations might be constrained by our location within regimes of truth, I believe it is necessary to begin this kind of moral inquiry (imagining how we might begin to respond creatively to moral situations of teaching and learning) in order to constitute a new politics of truth. Foucault's notion of morals does not seem to explicitly address the kinds of relationships we have with one another. Because schools are moral communities, it seems important to think about relationships within schools, especially the relationships between teachers and students.

Moral Understanding and Teacher-Student Relationships

In many instances, the teacher–student relationship has become a bureaucratized relationship (Davidson, 1996). Instead of asking, as van Manen (1990) suggests, "What is appropriate for this child in this situation?," school personnel rely on their systems of rules and regulations to inform their decisions. This is an example of how legislation and rule making is overemphasized as the key to moral life. As Mason (1999) notes, very often our protocols, and the time pressure exerted on us, leave us with little thought for the quality of the relations we have with one another. As discussed earlier, teachers, as much as students, seem to be caught in the machine of power described by Foucault (1980). Teachers, acting as bureaucrats in the machine of power, may find it difficult to make decisions in the best interests of their students. The limits of discourse place limits on the construction of subjectivities for teachers, as well as students. I appropriate Hepburn's (1997) assertion that the criticisms I develop are not directed at individual teachers but rather at the discursive constructions that shape their understandings and actions. When teachers act as bureaucrats rather than responding responsibly to their students, my criticism is directed at the institutional regime of truth that encourages and perpetuates this kind of teacher–student relationship. Teachers, as bureaucrats, often focus on the aspect of morals that Foucault (1982b) calls the moral code (prescriptions) imposed on people.

This model of moral understanding is described by Walker (1998) as the theoretical-juridical model, in which unilateral decisions and formulaic responses regiment moral consideration into fixed paths guaranteeing uniformity. It envisions impartial application of set policies to all, and best describes, says Walker (1998), participants in a structured game or institution. From Walker's description, it would seem that this model for moral understanding is currently in place in many schools. It is the model that a school's discipline policy is based upon, as it addresses the students in an institution as having fixed, stable and identical subject positions. This is an imagined position, much like the pejorative construction of youth as subjects of raging hormones (Roman, 1996). These imagined positions of youth are created by what Roman (1996) calls a moral panic—a manufactured crisis that justifies calls for regulating the alleged deviancy of adolescents. Acts of transgression, such as "going out of bounds in schools" or quietly leaving them (Roman, 1996), reinforce the notion that a moral panic is a real crisis. The transgressions that result from resistance to identity (e.g., skipping school, refusing to participate) are read as deviant, thus supporting the notion that further interventions are required to regulate adolescents. In the midst of a moral panic, it is difficult to constitute a new politics of truth. The participants in the moral community tend to be firmly entrenched in their respective positions.

In contrast to the theoretical-juridical model, Walker (1998) provides what she calls an expressive-collaborative view of moral understanding that views morality as "social negotiation in real time, where members of a community of roughly or largely shared moral belief try to refine understanding, extend consensus and eliminate conflict among themselves" (p. 64). In the expressive-collaborative model, eliminating conflict through moral reasoning takes a narrative form: "narratives are stories that show how a situation comes to be the particular problem it is, and that explore imaginatively the continuations that might resolve the problem and what they mean for the parties involved" (Walker, 1998, pp. 65–66). Rather than imposing uniformity in judgment and action (i.e., the Discipline Cycle) on acts of transgression, an attempt is made to replace communicative interaction. Fixed, stable, and singular subject positions are not assumed.

Returning once again to the story of Diane, the participant in this study who left school mid-year to begin her uphill battle with a Distance Education Program, I now interpret this as a striking example of an institutional response grounded firmly within a theoretical-juridical model of morality that seems to be taken for granted in the school. Using moral imagination (not blaming or castigating others) might have resulted in creative solutions to the problem of Diane's non-attendance. But much like being caught in the machine of power, teachers are caught within the hold of a theoretical-juridical model of moral understanding. Some teachers appear to be constrained by this model; that is, they are unable to imagine a relationship with their students not based on the impartial application of set policies. They assume that everyone in the institution makes similar moral judgments. Yet some teachers seem to recognize that moral claims upon them arise from their relationships with students whose interests are vulnerable to their actions and choices (Walker, 1998). These teachers seem to engage intuitively in an expressive-collaborative form of moral reasoning, carefully questioning their actions in relation to those who are vulnerable to them. To engage in this kind of moral inquiry is to go against the grain, and the reactions of school staff may be less than positive. Some teachers find themselves unable to work within a system that not only addresses students as having fixed and stable identities but also addresses teachers in a singular way. The fixed path of moral consideration and the impartial application of set policies are applied to teachers as well as to students.

Questioning the actions of the participants in a moral community is a kind of moral inquiry that is important, especially if we want to "directly interrogate some of the most morally troubling aspects of human social life: domination, oppression, exclusion, coercion, and basic disregard of some people by others" (Walker, 1998, p. 15). Inquiry is essentially a "moral activity because it focuses on the understandings we have of ourselves in relation to others and on the kind of society we would like to have" (Smith, 1992, p. 102). I would like to imagine a society and a school in which legislation and rule making are no longer over-emphasized. At the level of the school, this means reframing the teacher-student relationship from one that is essentially bureaucratized and paralyzed by a theoretical-juridical model of moral understanding.

Communicative interaction is required (Walker, 1998). This might take the form of "resuscitating" friendly teacher–student interactions, described by Devine (1996) as "chatting informally with students, challenging self-destructive behaviors, receiving student confidences, being in touch with the youth subculture" (p. 164). Cultivating an attitude of careful-caring attention (Mason, 1999) implies a commitment from teachers to listen to their students. Teachers not listening to student concerns was a frequently voiced complaint by the girls in this study:

> When teachers and students talk it's just about things that matter to the teacher. They just try to convince us to their way of thinking. That's what a conversation is between a teacher and a student. Like what has to be done in class and why it has to be done a certain way. And if you don't get it done and done their way, no one bothers to ask you why. (Rebecca: 02/17/99)

*   *   *   *

> You're not even allowed to talk about the things you normally talk about! The teachers just need to listen and try to look at it from a different point of view. They need to see things from our point of view. (Alicia: 06/22/98)

*   *   *   *

Similar results have been reported by Davidson (1996) and Taylor, Gilligan, and Sullivan (1995). In their study of 26 at-risk girls, Taylor et al. (1995) found that the participants said repeatedly that "nobody listens, nobody cares, nobody asks what they are thinking and feeling" (p. 1) and Davidson's (1996) participants said that "most adults do not take the time to hear or ask about the difficulties they face" (p. 10). The implications for resuscitating teacher–student relationships exceed the notion that teachers must simply be more sensitive to their students. As the above quotations show, communicative interaction around issues of curriculum (and the competing curricula in the social and cultural regimes) is also needed. Differences of experience, perception, and understanding between teachers and students create cultures of miscommunication and misunderstanding (Hargreaves, 1996), such as the following: "Mr. Green doesn't get anything. He doesn't understand. He knows I don't like gym but he doesn't even know why. He thinks I'm a bad ass" (Rebecca: 02/17/99). In this example, Rebecca is frustrated by what she perceives as Mr. Green's misconception of her actions and his failure to delve more deeply into the situation. She is refusing the subject position that she has been assigned—that of "bad ass."

Hargreaves (1996) says that it is "time to risk cacophony in our struggle to build authentic community" (p. 16). Building an authentic community means constructing alternative ground rules for communication and "building a coalition among the multiple, shifting, intersecting, and sometimes contradictory groups in the classroom" (Ellsworth, 1989, p. 317). The social curriculum needs to be altered to increase opportunities for students to envision themselves and others as not speaking always from the same subject position. From a feminist perspective, this means ensuring that female voices in the classroom are heard. In their study, Sadker and Sadker (1994) found that boys dominate discussions and interactions between teachers and students:

> Male students control classroom conversation. They ask and answer more questions. They receive more praise for the intellectual quality of their ideas. They get criticized. They get help when they are confused. They are the heart and center of interaction. (p. 42)

It is not sufficient, though, for teachers to simply provide a space for female voices. Educators also need to raise their own voices and, at times, challenge female and male adolescents' sometimes immature assumptions (Devine, 1996). This kind of challenging could, perhaps, begin to address the larger structures of domination that make possible systematically unequal relationships of power.

Buck and Ehlers (2002) encourage teachers to listen to adolescent girls and learn from them. This has implications for curriculum. In their study of designing science activities that engage adolescent girls in the curriculum, Buck and Ehlers determined that one of the criteria for designing engaging lessons in science was authenticity. That is, the science activity needed to directly respond to questions adolescent girls had about their world. It is not enough to simply listen to adolescent girls. Educators must take seriously the voices of girls and attempt to make curricular connections.

Educators also need to raise their voices when they hear student voices that demonstrate lack of respect and caring among peers. The complex social system that peers create for themselves is often filled with verbal harassment and other forms of psychological ill-treatment. Although most often occurring outside the teacher's gaze, voices engaging in these kinds of exclusionary practices must not be ignored. This is not to say that I am suggesting an even more pervasive form of the Panopticon, where every word and every action of every student is closely supervised. Students would undoubtedly find even more creative ways to avoid the institutional gaze. Yet the issue needs to be directly addressed in particular classrooms at particular times. Local struggles need local solutions, and using commercially prepared units of study that deal with bullying, for example, is not what I am advocating. Rather, I agree with Ellsworth (1989) and her suggestion of building a coalition among the multiple and contradictory groups in the classroom. Through these kinds of discussions, perhaps students will begin, as Hepburn (1997) says, to reconceptualize taken-for-granted aspects of "self" such as social identity "as something that we *do*, rather than something that we *have*, or something that we *are*" (p. 30). In other words, being popular, or a Loser or a Pathetic Wannabe, is not a fixed personality trait.

Again, there is a relationship to curriculum. Olafson and Latta (2002) found that students experience a greater sense of belonging when they engaged in school learning encounters involving creating, making, changing, and attending to difference. School tasks can be used to create a forum where issues of "otherness" can be taken up. When given the opportunity to address issues that matter to them, students can explore issues of identity (Olafson & Latta, 2002).

Broadly speaking, these institutional interventions are concerned largely with reconstituting, or "resuscitating," the teacher-student relationship in an expressive-collaborative model of moral understanding in order to avoid contributing to the moral panic of youth at risk. Most importantly, educators need to make sustained efforts to connect with adolescent girls. Attempts must also be made to connect girls with the mandated curriculum—attempts that address girls in ways that do not invoke a singular, stable, subject position that is identical for all students. Interventions are also needed in the cultural and social realms. As Currie (1999) notes, "If we are seriously interested in addressing the negative effects which cultural representations can have on young women, interventions in the social rather than simply the cultural realm are called for" (p. 302). In the next section I return to the particular, again using the example of physical education to illustrate how regimes of the body might be revisioned through specific practices in a particular location.

Revisioning Physical Education

I advocate for a physical education pedagogy (both social vision and practice) that remains specific to a particular context. In addition, physical education pedagogy must begin with the assumption that identities are made and not received. As Britzman (1991) notes, the work of curriculum is to incite identifications, not close them down. The curriculum possibilities raised by the participants within a specific context should not be taken as simple solutions to a complex phenomenon. The girls suggested that same-sex physical education classes, the elimination of spectacle, and a learner-centered program would increase their participation. It is important to note that none of the participants were highly skilled in physical education. These suggestions might not be appropriate for highly skilled and openly competitive girls who enjoy and actively seek out opportunities to be physically active, both at school and within the community.

Sex-segregated Classes

Sex-segregated classes were mentioned by the girls as an intervention that would possibly increase their attendance and enjoyment of physical education. Rebecca, for example, stated that "I'd be more interested in doing gym if it was an all-girls class and if there was a female teacher. I'd be more comfortable" (02/17/99), and Angela said, "I would love to have girls-only physical education. For one thing, you wouldn't have the boys getting all mad when the girls are better at something" (12/03/98).

Researchers have also recommended same-sex physical education classes. Jaffee and Manzer (1992), for example, noted that same-sex classes would provide a safe and uncritical environment where girls can play and try new activities. Although we have seen that girls can certainly be critical of one another in their social relationships, one advantage to same-sex classes is that the bodily comments made by boys would be absent. In this way, male discourses that define female bodies as objects and that sexually harass these bodies would be interrupted.

Same-sex physical education would be an ideal place to address what Gore (1993) believes is an absence of feminist pedagogy in schools. Physical education class is a relevant place to examine dominant cultural messages about female body image, sexuality and gender relations (O'Reilly, 1996). Feminist teachers in physical education could begin to emphasize how gendered knowledge and experience are produced (Gore, 1993). In Australia, for example, the physical education curriculum now includes critical analysis of the social construction of gendered bodies in and through sport and exercise (Kirk, 1997). But as O'Reilly's (1996) work demonstrates, the presence of female physical educators who are sympathetic to feminist issues does not ensure a program dedicated to critically examining or transforming problematic aspects of physical education. The participants in O'Reilly's study were constrained by powerful, historically situated and culturally sanctioned discourses privileging masculine interests in physical education.

Girls-only classes might also alleviate some of the cultural pressures to conform to certain standards of femininity. Angela alluded to this when she said that boys get mad if girls are better than boys at particular skills or sports. If physical education is no longer a place to show off for boys, perhaps girls like Raye, who maintained that she didn't like to sweat, might begin to see physical education as a place to achieve positive health benefits.

Eliminating Spectacle

Same-sex classes might also provide some relief from the male gaze; as Lynne mentioned: "I'd rather have girls-only P.E. because then you don't have men looking at you" (06/18/98). By "men," Lynne was referring to her teacher and her male classmates. Rebecca offered a solution to the problematic gazes incurred when doing a demonstration in front of the entire class, suggesting that students could perform their demonstrations "in front of a small group and not the entire class" (Rebecca: 02/17/99). The small groups that Rebecca suggested would consist of people in the same friendship groups. Relief from the surveillance of peers and criticism in the form of exclusionary tactics would be eliminated. Again, the male discourses and the discourses of exclusion could be interrupted within the practice of demonstrations. This is not to say that discourses of exclusion would not continue between various friendship groups. A student might not be criticized for her demonstration within her friendship group, but criticisms and other forms of verbal harassment would likely continue during other activities of physical education. As mentioned earlier, one of the tasks of educators is to become more attentive to these forms of exclusion in order to begin to interrupt them.

A Learner-Centered Program

The institutional games of physical education, the military-style form of exercise, and the focus on traditional sports were also problematic for many of the girls in this study. This traditional approach to physical education is based on a European, male, middle-class, sporting model (Ennis, 1995). Ennis found that a "multiactivity skills and sports curriculum with its preoccupations with regimented drill did not appear interesting" to her participants (p. 451). Hargreaves (1996) advocates what he calls reciprocal communication—that is, students need to be involved in innovations and have them explained. The "problems" of physical education need to be reframed in an expressive-collaborative model of moral reasoning, where communicative interaction (in this case about the curriculum of physical education) can take place. Alicia provided a concrete suggestion for a form of reciprocal communication in physical education where students could be offered choices in the curriculum:

> They could offer you a choice of sports and activities to do in the fall and you could select what you were interested in and then do what you want. It would make it more fun. They could just teach us how to play and then we'd be fine. We'd just play badminton or basketball or whatever. And we wouldn't have to know stuff like the velocity of the ball and get tested on the rules. And we wouldn't have to get our parents to write us notes so that we could miss gym. (Alicia: 06/22/98)

Alicia sees the element of choice as removing one of the obstacles to physical education. A curriculum that responds to the needs and interests of students, and students being actively involved in structuring the curriculum, might increase interest and enjoyment in physical education. It would also provide teachers with the opportunity to address their students in ways that do not invoke the stable, unified and identical conception of identity that seems to invite resistance.

According to Ennis (1995), teachers and students need to "negotiate a shared vision in which both groups contribute to an educational approach to physical education" (p. 456). With a range of choices and a curriculum based on a model other than the European, male, middle-class model, students could enter into the games of physical education on terms more of their own making. Curricular alternatives such as programs based on personal fitness or on helping students experience a "range of physical activities that focus on learning skills necessary to engage in active, healthy lifestyles across their life spans" (Ennis, 1995, p. 458) might be appealing to adolescent girls.

Based on the results of their study, Jaffe and Manzer (1992) advocate decreasing the competitive aspect of physical education. They found that girls are more likely to participate when the focus is on self-esteem, skill building and teamwork. In the following comment, Raye confirmed that many girls dislike the competitive aspect of physical education: "Girls hate phys. ed. because of the competitive part of it. You always have to try to be better than someone else" (11/25/98).

These interventions in physical education are but small steps. A feminist educator working with girls in a subject area explicitly concerned about the body could begin to develop among her students a critical stance to the ways their bodies have been constructed through the regimes of the body, and she could begin to disrupt some of their taken-for-granted understandings about living in a female body in a patriarchal world. Although I make these suggestions in the context of physical education classes, they might be appropriate in other subject areas. Using the expressive-collaborative model of moral reasoning to frame "problems" of adolescence and discuss solutions seems a more reasonable way for the members of a moral community to sensibly and collaboratively determine how they can go on together in shared terms. The desire to actively construct subjectivity in particular ways (the ethical aspect of regime of truth) and to refuse the submission of subjectivity is a key element in this moral community. What is needed are forms of address within the curriculums of the regimes of the body that open up the range of subject positions available to adolescent girls.

Everything is Dangerous

The interventions suggested do not represent the final word on how feminist educators might open up the range of possibilities for adolescent girls. As noted earlier, everything is dangerous according to Foucault (1982a). Increasing the range of possibilities does not necessarily mean that all possibilities will be positive. Given the opportunity and the encouragement to create alternative subject positions, some adolescent girls might envision potentially destructive subjectivities. As girls choose to be the subjects rather than the objects of power relationships, they may increasingly become the perpetrators of verbal and physical violence (see, for example, *Odd Girl Out: The Hidden Culture of Aggression in Girls* by Rachel Simmons, 2003). Negative experiences with power relationships (the experience of power in its most arbitrary and useless forms) may encourage young people "to seek to reestablish their own position of dominance through violence" (Epp, 1997, p. 27). I am thinking here of Alicia, whose mother admitted that Alicia had been physically violent with her.

Distance education as a means of escaping the institutional and social regimes of the school is not without its dangers either. Without the specter of responsible and caring adult guidance, students may choose to do nothing. Rebecca informed me, for example, that neither Alicia nor Diane was managing to complete her schoolwork in the distance program. In a Distance Program, the mandated curriculum is no different from that taught in the schools. If anything, a Distance Program is more restrictive, in that no opportunity exists to alter the way the curriculum addresses the students. Although free from the harassment of peer groups at school, Alicia and Diane reportedly spend most of their time on the street with a peer group whose common denominator is school non-attendance. I suspect that this peer group has developed a set of social rules that are nearly as constraining as those found in the school. The "freedom" that Alicia and Diane find outside of school is a form of submission to subjectivity, although different from those found within the school. Their escape from one social regime has led them to an alternative social regime where their desires for acceptance and belonging can be met.

There are no easy answers for increasing the range of possibilities for adolescent girls, but according to Bordo (1997) this does not mean that we must become fatalistic and passive:

> To act responsibly and with hope, it's not necessary that we know the final outcome of our actions. We assess what we take to be the chief dangers or needs of a situation—the practices that require demystification, criticism, transformation—and we act, both individually and collectively, ready to change course if we discover something that we didn't notice at the outset or something that has emerged since we began. (p. 191)

Like Taylor et al. (1995), I have found the practice of inquiry, especially interviewing, to be a practice of relationship: "The interviews demonstrate that when women approach girls as authorities on their own experience and listen to them intently and with respect, girls can speak openly about their thoughts and feelings" (Taylor et al., 1995, p. 128). As a concerned (feminist) adult in the community, I intend to act responsibly and with hope and to continue to practice my inquiry as a practice of relationship with adolescent girls.

appendix

Reconstructed Life Stories

● ●

Alicia's Reconstructed Life Story

Individuality is something that I really value. I see myself as an individual. Everybody is different. Some people show it more than others. I'm not really concerned about what other people think. I found that out the hard way. I had an identity crisis. It was hell. I was unhappy. I just didn't know who to be. I didn't know how to act. I didn't know what to say and I didn't know what people would think but I just realized who cares what they think because they are thinking the exact same thing. When you try too hard to fit in it doesn't work. Last year, I had like no friends. Last year the peer thing was pretty bad—like last year nobody liked me, everybody had something against me, and I was so self-conscious. I remember last year almost every night I would go home crying because somebody would make fun of me all day. I didn't how to act because no matter what I did somebody would make fun of me and I was only trying to be myself. And like I always cared what they thought because I always thought oh they're cool, I've got to follow them but this year I just really don't care. Okay, I tried to dress like them one time. I want shopping and I tried on the clothes right and I was just standing in the mirror thinking I look like them. I just thought I don't want to look like them. So I didn't buy the stuff. It's hard to maintain an identity when the push to be alike. This year I don't really care. I have lots of friends. I've gained tons. I value intelligence and people that you can like talk to.

I stopped coming to school after Christmas. I don't know why. Part of it is all the rules and regulations. Just like one long weekend, I went back and I just wasn't motivated to go. It was such a drag. I can't really explain it. It's such a hassle. I'm not thinking about dropping out. It's dumb. I think it would be a lot better if you were just given a whole bunch of work for one day; get it all done and then you can leave when you get it done. Like say it's noon or whatever and when it comes to three o'clock you could just take it home. That would be better. There's just no point in sitting there doing nothing. So there's the time factor as well and kind of being held captive for six hours a day. I was just like not motivated to come. It's not the work. I love learning. Like I said I was bored so I learned Spanish over the internet when I was at home. There's nothing else to do. It's not the work at all. But the home environment wasn't really working either because I just kind of got lazy with this schoolwork. I got all the work done. I just didn't want to come. There is a different kind of freedom if you're not in school because you don't have to care about what you're wearing, if your clothes match, or whatever. Not like I'm really worried about the kind of stuff but you just never have to worry about it at all if you're at home. And you can concentrate, there's nothing else on your mind. But then I decided to come back to school. It's stupid to miss so much school. I've been away for a couple of weeks or a week and a half or so. I just couldn't miss anymore. First of all there is nothing to do and I kept worrying about am I going to screw up my future and everything. There's no point in not coming. So I made the decision on my own.

I like it better now that I'm doing this independent program. I don't mind sitting in the library working on my own. I like it better than the classroom. It's not the work. The work can be boring but that's work, it's work right. It's just the environment. Everybody's at each others' throats. Not like on the outside but on the inside. The school is just a bad environment. It kind of pushes you away. More than the hassle of coming here, it's the hassle of everybody being stupid around you. Like you're having an argument or some gossip went around or childish crap like that, it's stupid. You can't learn that way with people being stupid around you. Everybody at this school hates somebody. Everybody here is childish, I think. Not everybody but 90% of the people. Sometimes I feel like an outsider on the inside. I'm not here to hate people. It's frustrating. It's just really pathetic and pointless. I think everybody in this school should just like lay back a little bit. Don't be so tense.

There's like the people who are so cool and the people who are cool but nobody realizes that they are cool. I'm in the second group. Because people in the first group are so unopen minded that it's not even funny. They just think that if you don't dress like me then you're not cool. The kids that think they're so cool—don't feel confident about themselves. They have to keep the attention on themselves.

I want to go to law school. I don't want to be a housewife. It would be boring, first of all. I could do better than that. And the thing is it's so degrading. It's like saying that men are better than us. I don't believe that. Not at all.

Diane's Reconstructed Life Story

When I was in elementary, people used to tease me for whatever reason they could, and I thought to myself that I was so young and I had a low self-esteem. And then when I got to junior high, I matured. And I have higher self-esteem and I don't need them to boss me around. If you fight back for yourself and you stand up for yourself, they realize that you don't care then they won't do anything. But if you just sit there and ignore them, they'll think that they're putting you down.

The teachers are more strict than in the earlier grades. And it's harder when the teachers are strict. We don't suck up to the teachers. We just do our work and whatever. But other people that suck up to the teachers, they get favored. I don't like going up in front of the class and doing stuff on the board. Why do they do that anyway? If you don't want to do something and they know you don't, they shouldn't do that to you. And then they act like you're stupid. And I don't like phys. ed. Running around the gym 10,000 times. Have fun, and sing and dance, and put your finger on your nose and toes outwards, backwards.

We call the popular people the Snob Squad. That's all the girls that think they're the best and everything and they think everything revolves around them and that everybody cares about them so much, but I don't. They think all the same. So they won't get made fun of. It's easy to outsmart them; they're Ditzes. They don't, like, know anything, they just think they do. And they're not even that popular. They'd better enjoy this year because it's not going to last. It's a dream. Popularity and stuff. When they get to high school, they're going to have so many enemies. They're going to get their butts kicked.

The Wannabes are all the people that try to act like the popular group by like dressing like it or calling themselves cool. The Snob Squad doesn't let them in because they're not good enough. And then there's a large range of people that are different from everyone else in the school that I would classify as independent. They're like people who have friends in school but they don't care if they're popular or not. Like me. I'm just here for the work. Like we don't care if we're popular or not in this school. I'm not really into the social scene here. They're not ones to socialize with. They think we're druggies. I don't know why. We hang around with other people and some of them are druggies, but I don't know how they would know that. I don't know where they got the idea to call us druggies. Maybe because we're not trying to socialize with anybody. We're not druggies.

Now I'm being home-schooled, but I still see my friends after school. It's because I didn't get along with any of the teachers and because Rebecca got moved to a different classroom. When she first moved it wasn't a problem. But then Mrs. White knew that I was upset. She wouldn't look me in the eye; she ignored me and wouldn't answer my questions. Now I've got no one. With no friends, I can't stand up for myself. I guess the teachers cared more about Rebecca than me. And Mr. Craig didn't care about anyone. I think that I'd like to go the alternative high school for high school.

Brenda's Reconstructed Life Story

Being popular is different in different schools. In my old school, I was popular. I was in the popular group and then I moved here and

I wasn't. That was really hard. But I was popular when I first came. Now I'm in the middle.

Being popular means being accepted. A lot of people, like in this school think like if you're not popular, you're a loser. People in the popular group think that if you're not popular, you're a loser. Part of being popular is being attractive to boys and having boys in your group with you. But sometimes, it doesn't work like that. Like Jayne, she came to our school and she has the nicest clothes, the nicest hair, she's really pretty, and they hated it because she was better than them sort of. She was too perfect and so they didn't like it. But she was actually really nice. She's a loser to a lot of people. Being popular also has a lot to do with sports. Sports is a big factor. Like all the girls, jocks, or whatever you want to call them, like they are popular. And it's because guys can relate to them right, because a lot of guys are into sports right. Usually when you do a lot of sports, you're skinnier and you've got a higher self esteem and stuff. The perfect Grade 7 girl would be like skinny, narrow shoulders, small waist, long legs, strong big chest, small ears, small nose, straight white teeth, interesting eyes, oval face, no zits, blemishes, scars, or facial hair. If you had the image you would probably be popular.

The popular group is probably the biggest group and they hang out with the guys and they all dress cool. I'm not really one of them. Like I hang out with a couple of them, but I'm not in the popular group. They kind of group together and they exclude other people. There's some people in the popular group that you can't associate with unless you're with them, then they're totally jerks. There's sort of sections of the popular group. I think there's four or five.

The Pathetic Wannabe's are the people who follow the popular people around. Like Margaret, she follows them around and everybody hates her, and everybody talks behind her back. They say mean things. But I think she knows; she just really wants to be cool and she thinks that if I stick with them long enough, they're going to like me but, they're really starting to hate her more. And then there's the Skids. I think of them as druggies because I know they have done drugs, I'm certain of it, and I don't want to hang out with them because I don't want to get into that stuff. They would be in the middle, between loser and the middle.

The loser group is really quiet and they don't care about sports and stuff, don't try to get in any activity, and they're very judgmental. They see you and they're going, oh, you're not one of us. They really stick together. I swear they've got this vow, don't give any money or anything to anybody. I don't really know them. There's a few of them but I don't talk to them at all. I'm not friends with them and they don't want to talk to me. They would probably ignore me anyhow. I think it's because people are rude to them and they think that you're going to be mean to them even if you walk up. The loser group's fashions are hideous. They're awful—stretch pants that go around your feet and then the pants that go tight at the bottom.

The different groups have different ways of excluding. Like the loser group, I don't blame them actually, because we're all jerks. Like every one of us has said something. I'll admit it, I've probably said something mean. The loser groups are mean to others. Because nobody likes them. Like I said, I would be that way too. If people walked up to me and said those things, I wouldn't want to talk to them either.

The popular group does the brush off, the cold shoulder. That's usually how they do it. They're usually not mean about it, they usually just sort of walk off. And they stand in a circle a lot to like keep people out. I don't think they do it on purpose. Like if somebody comes really close to you, you don't really mean to move back, it's just that it happens. And then they never say something to their faces, it's behind their back. The popular group isn't mean to your face.

I'm really self conscious about my legs. Myself, I have scary, scary legs. I have longer legs, but I have white legs and I wouldn't show them to anyone. Because they're white, and they're ugly. People might come up to me and say, white legs, eh? And they would be joking around and stuff, but it's really true. In Phys. Ed. I'm not good at gymnastics and my legs flop all over the place. I don't like going up in front of a class because I shake. My hands shake, like my whole body, I don't know why. And then when I go up in front of the classroom, when they're all together, I just shake and sometimes I'm like, and it's really, I'm not afraid of them, I can't help it. I'm thinking to myself, why am I shaking? I can't help it. I don't know why I do it. Doing like a demo in phys. ed.—it's been sort of embarrassing.

Like once I was shaking so much, my head started shaking. I've been made fun of in gym. Because I look funny when I run, I've heard. I don't know how they mean it, if it's insulting or joking, but I don't care. It's not like a big deal to me.

Rebecca's Reconstructed Life Story

I was really bad in Grade 6. I got like all Ds. In Grade 6 I had no friends in my class and I didn't work because I didn't feel comfortable working, and since I did bad in everything, then they thought I must be a druggie, a pothead or whatever, a bad ass. I think the teachers thought that too.

The quality of my work is worse than this year. I don't like the class, the teacher, it's everything. She's too strict, they expect you to know everything, say it in front of the class if you get it or not, and I don't like doing that, and that's about it. They expect you to know everything, and they just put the work on your shoulder and expect you to do it. The assignments pile up. In math and science, I don't understand a whole lot, so I've got a C and a D. I'm not getting things in science because I don't ask him questions that I don't get. Mr. Craig asks me a question; I feel stupid because I don't get it. He explains it in front of the whole class, and then he asks if you have any questions or if you don't get it, and that's all he does. I don't like it. I don't understand it. I don't know where I go wrong. And I don't feel comfortable asking questions in class. They'll think I'm stupid. I don't raise my hand and tell the teacher that I don't understand. It would be like saying, "Look at me, I'm stupid." I can't do my work because I don't understand; then you're like stressed because you don't get it.

Mr. Day caught me in the library a few days ago for skipping gym.And he said I might get an out-school suspension if I keep this up. I don't think we could negotiate some kind of a plan that would work for both of us. He said he was going to bring it up with the assistant principal, and he'll make up a punishment or something. Like an in-school suspension or an out-school suspension or something. And I don't want to participate. They just tell me I have to. And I just say I don't want to. I don't like gym. I don't like the competition stuff and I don't like doing the performances in front of the group because then you get all the stupid comments afterwards. I'd feel more comfortable in phys. ed. if it was just girls and a smaller group. The boys, they have a big mouth. The boys insult the girls but the girls don't insult the boys. It's just so complicated; I just don't want to deal with it anymore.

The teachers won't listen to your point of view. They just try to convince you to think like them. They just don't get it. Never in my school career have I come across a teacher who was interested in getting it. Never has there been a teacher that I could talk to. It would help if teachers would talk to us about stuff that matters to us, not just the stuff that matters to them. All the teachers talk about it: well you have to get this done, and you have to get this done, and you have to be here to get it done, and if you don't then you get a zero. And nobody asks why you're not getting it done. They don't ask why. They just tell you, if you don't, then it's your loss, no more for you.

The Snob Squad they dress like with all tight clothes and stuff to show off their bodies and stuff. And they want the guys, so that's like the whole point. That's what they do it for, the guys. I don't understand why. They're flogging themselves over the guys they know. So the girls just do that to make the guys want to like them because that's the whole point. With no guys, they would be nothing. That's why they act like snobby and they make fun of people, to show off in front of the guys. So the guys will notice them and then the guys will think they're cool because they do that or whatever. That's how it works around here. They've never said anything mean to me really. They must have seen me with my friends or something and they know that I have a lot more friends then they do. But they still act like they're the best but they don't like say anything. But the guys harass me. They just say stupid things. And it doesn't mean anything to me what they say anymore because I know I'm better than them.

The loser groups are at the bottom of the pile in terms of status. They work too hard in school. They care about their work too much and they don't have any room for like socializing with other people, communicating.

I got switched to a new home room and that's why Diane doesn't want to come, because she's by herself now in her class without a friend. She doesn't feel comfortable there. Because she needs a friend to stick up for her and stuff. People like, say stuff. Everybody does it. They just make comments and stuff. Put you down. Mean comments. Like they make fun of Diane's ears. They're big. Most of the time the comments come from the boys. Sometimes the girls do it. If you're by yourself, it's hard to stick up for yourself, you need backup. With two you can stand up, but with one you can't. That's kind of what happened to Diane. She was left as one and so she had no backup, and that's why she's not here anymore.

My dream would be to have seven people in a class, seven people who were all my friends, and then teachers wouldn't be really competitive, you'd be working together. You'd have more fun, like get how to do it and the teacher would have more time too. The small group is what I need. I just want to get the work done and get it done fast, and I want to understand it. I want to graduate and then I want to maybe go to university or college. I think it will be better in university because everyone is more mature and stuff. And you wouldn't care if you had friends either. You might be by yourself and get your work done and no one will care.

Raye's Reconstructed Life Story

Like one year, like in Grade 6, I tried to kill myself because I just thought everybody hated me because like this one person that was sort of popular, that I wanted to like me, she's just like, you know, you're so annoying, you're really ugly, no wonder everybody hates you and you're just like such a bitch. And I was devastated; I'm just like, well what did I do, I was just trying to stick up for myself. Then like a guy started calling all of his friends and his friends told their friends and their friends like told some of the popular people, then they automatically just started making fun of me and everything.

Last year I was just trying to hard to fit in, but now I'm like, okay, if they accept me, they're my friends, but if they're not, they're not. Big deal. And it's just I'm kind of being nicer to people and I'm trying to control my temper. I feel worthy to be popular now because I think I have a better attitude; I know there's some things that I could work on. I'm definitely having a better year in terms of being accepted. And I guess it sort of changed because when I came at the beginning of the year, everybody was being so much nicer to me. I sort of changed my attitude and like I changed my outlook on life and I just changed a lot about my personality, and with my new personality, of course, I had to update my clothes, so I bought some new stuff. It's kind of like more in and relaxed. Things are going better because I'm being accepted more and people are just generally being nicer to me.

Well everybody pretty much knows who's in the popular group and who isn't. It's just usually by the way they look. Like some people carry themselves with more confidence because they know they're popular. They can pretty much say whatever they want and nobody will do anything about it. Like if you just watch anybody in this school that's popular you can see that there's just something about them that just lets you, like automatically right off, know they're popular. It's just like an unspoken thing.

That's the only thing that I don't like about popularity is because you never know when your life is going to change. Usually when you get dropped by one group, like you can't exactly go back into it. Like if you get dropped from the popular group, like, nobody is ever popular again. Because you can even look at somebody wrong and the next day you're going to be like the most hated person in the entire world. You have to be really careful about what you say, how you say it, who you say it to.

Aside from the popular people we mostly have like skaters. And even though the skaters are kind of in a group of their own, like they're still really popular, like with the popular people and everything, like they pretty much intertwine. The only thing that really separates them is their hobbies and their clothing, but other than that, they're pretty much the same. In between prep and skater group is another group because like they dress in the loose comfortable clothing, but they still have standardized popular stuff. And then there's like the jock dressers who I really hate. They're the people that dress in all brand name sports stuff like they wear jerseys all the time and stuff like that. Probably the least popular people are just like the wannabes or the losers, the loners and stuff like that. They kind of group together. The popular people just sort of put them all in one group because they're not really in between, but most of them aren't like exactly right on the bottom. So like they just shove them all together in this one big clump of three different categories, and they're just like the bottom of the pile. These are the bottom dwellers.

I think the most subtle ways to exclude people is like to say, "Oh yeah, well I have to get class now otherwise I'm going to be late," and it's like the middle of lunch or whatever, and you just take off. That's probably like the subtlest way you can pull it off. When it's in between is when you're talking to somebody that you don't really want to and then you just see somebody walking down the hall, like anybody that you like hanging around with better than that person, it's like, "Excuse me, I have to go talk to them." But I think the worst way to tell somebody that you're mad at them is like, "Oh just leave me alone okay, I just hate your guts; I don't want you to even look at me."

Guys like the big chest, like girls don't really care unless they get really, like unless they get like into their junior of high school or whatever, and they're still flat, then they're going to start to get kind of peeved. Like with girls, like they think it's kind of weird if you've got like too big of a chest, but the guys are like, yea, the bigger, the better. Guys are horny. People like at first glance, if they haven't heard a lot about your personality, like even if they have, usually they judge you by what you look like. Like if you look okay when you first meet somebody and they've heard about you, then it's like, oh yea, their looks sort of fit their personality; maybe they've got new stuff that I'd want to find out. I'm not really embarrassed about my appearance, I'm just sort of. I'm 5'8". I don't want to be that tall. And all the popular girls are about six inches shorter than me. And it just makes me feel kind of weird. Everybody on both sides of my family has really big bones. I've tried to lose weight in a hurry. I don't like using a laxative. That's disgusting. After taking them for a while, it's like hey, I'm not losing hardly any weight at all, and it's just making me feel disgusting. And for a while, like I just don't eat as much as I normally did, and you know how people say, oh yea, if you don't eat what you're supposed to, then you're just going to get sick. Well I felt fine. Every once in a while my stomach would growl and I'm just like, I'm not hungry. And so I'd only eat when it was offered to me.

I think girls really hate phys. ed. because people are always trying to do better than everybody else—the competitive part of it. Girls like to show off, especially if there's like a guy that they like or think is cute or whatever, they want to be able to show them that they're on their level. The best Teen magazine or whatever that gives you advice on flirting or whatever, they even tell you to like subtly copy the movements of your crush so you can show that you're on the same wave length. But they also say that instead of, like directly approaching the guy that you have the crush on, like give them a chance to come to you. It's an elaborate game. Phys. ed. is a chance to kind of show off for anybody of the opposite sex. Girls don't want to demonstrate because they're just sort of embarrassed of doing something dumb. Like guys are expected to be juvenile so it doesn't really matter. But girls, like they're expected to be like graceful, always in control, be able to do basically everything. Even if a girl gets like a red face from running too much, they're expected to always be like calm and be able to always look good, like all the time, but if you have like a really red sweaty face, like the guys are just like, ooh yuck, what have you been doing. Like for girls, like b.o. and all that kind of stuff is like, kind of a form of asparagus or something, it's like keep away. There are some girls that try to work hard in phys. ed. I think it's weird. It's like something that comes with being popular. Because the popular girls seem to look good all the time. They can be running for like about an hour and a half, and like their faces aren't red, they might be breathing hard, but they look perfectly fine, right. I don't really like sweating at all because it just makes me feel kind of run down and tired.

August's Reconstructed Life Story

I used to be a geek last year in grade seven but now I'm not. I changed my attitude. My friends said, "If you're going to act like a bitch then we aren't going to be your friends." So I smartened up and got dressed like a skater, cool. And I like the way I look now even if no one else does. If no one else does, that is your problem, deal with it. I don't care how I look but I've put myself on a diet before. I don't eat hardly because what is the point?

So this year I am in the Skater group. All my skater friends wear ripped up jeans, baggy pants, and short hair. I am like a fine mama. Now I know so many grade niners it's not funny. Other groups at school are the geeks, the sluts, and the jocks. Most guys like girls in short skirts. They like make-up and all that. Some guys just like girls for what they look like, not their personality. Some girls like to dress up and be a slut. Like short mini skirts, halter tops and big heels. They shave their legs and lot and they are skinny. And they have rude attitudes. Like the models in magazines. They are sex objects and they wear sluttish clothes. That's not fair to us. Why should we try to do that? We should try to put on halter tops and mini skirts and heels. And walk around for a whole entire day. My mom thinks that I should look like one of those girls. The girls that are not sluts like to play sports, like the skaters and they won't go into bed with a guy.

What bugs me most about school is that people get into physical fights and want to fight me. Like today in gym I was standing in the middle and I threw the basketball and it bounced off the floor. Then it hit Michelle in the head. She came up to me and kicked me and I scratched her. I broke her nail by mistake and she came back to me. So we started a fight. And now she wants to fight me after school today, bitch-slapping and all that. There's lots of stuff at schools that the teachers don't know about. Like there is going to be a big rally after school today, a big humungous fight. And I am going to kick the shit out of Steve.

It takes quite a lot of work to keep track of who is going out with who and who dumped who. But I keep my mouth shut so I don't get the shit kicked out of me. Starting rumors is something that can get you in trouble. But I've been beaten up tons of times, and now I've learned that it's better to keep my mouth shut.

I've had three boyfriends this year. And now Nick wants to marry me. He thought I was nineteen, but I'm only fourteen and you have to be eighteen to get married. But I'm not going to get married right away anyhow because I want to live my life. When I'm going to get a husband I want to see other guys to see which one is better.

I'm not too worried about final exams this year. I'm ready for them, but I don't know if I'm going to do well. If I don't study I do good at them. If I do study then I do bad. I wish that I was gone. I don't like grade 8. I like grade 10. I think that I would have a better year if I could go to grade 10 because all my friends are there and I could get more work done.

Lynne's Reconstructed Life Story

I found moving to junior high really stressful. I didn't even know what to expect. I was scared about getting a reputation. In grade seven last year, I didn't even know that I had bad marks at first. It was a shock when I saw the report card and after lunch I hid it under my bed. I was scared of what my dad was going to say. I just didn't understand what the teachers were asking for and I thought, "who cares how I feel about that?" And I didn't ask any teachers for help because I was scared of what they were going to think of me and I didn't want to look bad. If you don't understand you have to try to hide it.

I miss a lot of school but it's not because I want to. I miss school when I'm needed at home. I try to help out as much as I can, especially now that my dad's been laid off. Last year, Mom was sick and she called the school and they came and told me. I ran to my locker and grabbed everything and I ran out. If my mom needs me I'll come running home.

Danielle cut my hair in class and I didn't even notice. I thought she was playing with my hair. Then I reached up and I'm like, what the hell is going on? I just cried. I had to get the rest of my hair cut that night. She got suspended for that. Danielle's tougher than me; I do not want to fight. The rest of the kids in the class really supported me. I'm not a fighter, but if my other friends are in a fight, and they need help, I will go in there, and they'll get bleeding noses. There's a group of girls at school that are the trouble-maker girls. They hurt you and do mean things to you, and say, "You'd better be careful or something will happen to you." And there's the goody-goody girls. Just because I get my work done, doesn't mean I'm a goody-goody. I was never, ever popular. I was popular around my friends. Even in the classroom right now I'm popular only because I'm helping when the teachers aren't there and I know the answer.

Phys. ed. I don't like, especially demonstrations in front of the whole class and there's a whole bunch of eyes staring at you. I didn't mind in grade four, but now, it's like "Oh God, help me" and I turn all red. I'd rather have girls-only p.e. classes because then you don't have men looking at you. It would be a whole different atmosphere. A female teacher would understand what I was going through, but boys don't' understand because they're men. They're stupid and they don't understand. Like they don't know about the emotional pain and then they put more pain on us. If I could change anything about this school, it would be the boys. Some of them are really, really nice, but most boys are a pain in the butt. They just don't do their work and they're name-callers. The boys do it when the teacher isn't listening.

I am scared about my final report card. I want to do my best. I don't know about the kinds of courses I want to take in high school but I want to finish grade twelve. I promised my grandma that I would finish school and then I want to get a good job.

Emma's Reconstructed Life Story

There's more freedom in elementary school than in junior high. Everyone, including the teachers, thinks that teenagers are bad. Like in stores, people think teenagers are dangerous because they steal. Probably adults steal more than teenagers. But teenagers have the bad reputation. At school, people are always judged on their appearance. In elementary school, you don't really care what you look like. Here, everyone wants to be like everyone else.

There's a dress code at this school. You're not allowed to wear certain things. But it's mostly girls' clothes that the rules are about and that's not fair. Boys can wear anything they want. But we can't wear stuff they say is sluttish. If you wear something like a belly shirt then people will say stuff about you, like you'll get called a slut. But boys are never sluttish.

I like doing projects at school because it's more fun that just sitting at your desk and writing and writing and writing. I don't like French, but even if I don't like being there I just do the work anyways, I just keep quiet and put up with it. I don't cause any trouble, but some kids do if they don't want to be in a class. They fight with the teachers over the work. So you can either shut up and do the work, put up a fight or just sit there and do nothing.

I would like to do better at school next year. I am just past the passing marks now. I can do the work but I hand stuff in late so I'm going to have to be on time with the big projects. I want to be a model when I grow up. I wanted to just like them—skinny. But I need to be taller. I'm naturally skinny, and the guys like me because I'm skinny.

Bibliography

●　●

AAUW. (1992). *The AAUW report: How schools shortchange girls.* Report by Wellesley College Center for Research on Women. Washington, DC: American Association of University Women and National Education Association.

Abowitz, K.K. (2000). A pragmatist revisioning of resistance theory. *American Educational Research Journal, 37*(4), 897–907.

Adler, P. & Adler, P. (1997). Parent-as-researcher: The politics of researching in the personal life. In R. Hertz (Ed.), *Reflexivity and voice.* Thousand Oaks: Sage.

Alder, N. & Moulton, M. (1998). Caring relationships: Perspectives from middle school students. *Research in Middle Level Quarterly, 21*(3), 15–32.

Allen, A. (1996). Foucault on power: A theory for feminists. In S. Hekman (Ed.), *Feminist interpretations of Michel Foucault.* University Park, PA: The Pennsylvania State University Press.

Alpert, B. (1991). Students' resistance in the classroom. *Anthropology and Education Quarterly, 22,* 350–366.

Bakhtin, M. (1968). *Rabelais and his world.* (H. Iwolsky, Trans.). Bloomington, IL: Indiana University Press.

Ball, D. & Wilson, S. (1996). Integrity in teaching: Recognizing the fusion of the moral and intellectual. *American Educational Research Journal, 33*(1), 155–192.

Bartky, S. (1990). *Femininity and domination: Studies in the phenomenology of oppression.* New York: Routledge.

Becker, H. (1986). *Writing for social scientists: How to start and finish your thesis, book, or article.* Chicago: University of Chicago Press.

Belsey, C. (1980). *Critical practice.* London: Methuen.

Bennett, K. & LeCompte, M. (1990). *The way schools work: A sociological analysis of education.* New York: Longman.

Bibby, R. & Posterski, D. (1992) *Teen trends: A nation in motion.* Toronto: Stoddart.

Bogdan, B.C., & Biklen, S.K. (2003). *Qualitative research for education: An introduction to theories and methods.* Boston, MA: Pearson.

Bordo, S. (1993). *Unbearable weight: Feminism, Western culture and the body.* Berkeley: University of California Press.

Bordo, S. (1997). *Twilight zones: The hidden life of cultural images from Plato to O.J.* Los Angeles: University of California Press.

Bowles, S. & Gintis, H. (1976). *Schooling in capitalist America.* New York: Basic Books.

Britzman, D. (1991). *Practice makes practice: A critical study of learning to teach.* New York: State University of New York Press.

Britzman, D. (1998). *Lost subjects, contested objects: Toward a psychoanalytic inquiry of learning.* New York: SUNY Press.

Brumberg, J. (1997). *The body project: An intimate history of American girls.* New York: Vintage Books.

Buck, G., & Ehlers, N. (2002). Four criteria for engaging girls in the middle level classroom. *Middle School Journal, 34*(1), 48–53.

Chepaytor-Thomson, R., & Ennis, C. (1997). Reproduction and resistance to the culture of femininity and masculinity in secondary school physical education. *Research Quarterly for Exercise and Sport, 68*(1), 89–99.

Clifton, R. & Roberts, L. (1993). *Authority in classrooms.* Scarborough, ON: Prentice Hall.

Collins, J. (1995). *Discourse and resistance in urban elementary classrooms: A poststructuralist perspective.* Paper presented at the annual meeting of the American Educational Research Association (San Francisco, CA).

Contenta, S. (1993). *Rituals of failure: What schools really teach.* Toronto: Between the Lines.

Creswell, J.W. (1998). *Qualitative inquiry and research design: Choosing among the five traditions.* Thousand Oaks, CA: Sage.

Currie, D. (1999). *Girl talk: Adolescent magazines and their readers.* Toronto: University of Toronto Press.

Davidson, A. (1996). *Making and molding identity in schools: Student narratives on race, gender, and academic engagement.* New York: State University of New York Press.

Davies, B. (1992). Women's subjectivity and feminist stories. In C. Ellis and M. Flaherty (Eds.), *Investigating subjectivity: Research on lived experience.* London: Sage.

Davies, B. (1993). *Shards of glass: Children reading and writing beyond gendered identities.* Cresshill, NJ: Hampton Press.

Davies, B. and Harre, R. (1990). Positioning: The discursive production of selves. *Journal for the Theory of Social Behavior, 20*(1), 43–63.

Debold, E. (1995). Helping girls survive the middle grades. *Principal,* January, 22–24.

Devine, J. (1996). *Maximum security: The culture of violence in inner-city schools.* Chicago: The University of Chicago Press.

Dyer, G. & Tiggemann, M. (1996). The effects of school environment on body concerns in adolescent women. *Sex Roles, 34*(1/2), 127–138.

Eisenhart, M. (1998). On the subject of interpretive reviews. *Review of Educational Research, 68*(4), 391–399.

Ellsworth, E. (1989). Why doesn't this feel empowering? *Harvard Educational Review, 59,* 297–324.

Ellsworth, E. (1997). *Teaching positions: Difference, pedagogy, and the power of address.* New York: Teachers College Press.

Ennis, C. (1995). Teachers' responses to noncompliant students: The realities and consequences of a negotiated curriculum. *Teaching and Teacher Education, 11*(5), 445–460.

Epp, J. (1996). Schools, complicity and sources of violence. In J. Epp & A. Watkinson (Eds.), *Systemic violence: How schools hurt children.* London: The Falmer Press.

Epp, J. (1997). Authority, pedagogy, and violence. In J. Epp and A. Watkinson (Eds.), *Systemic violence in education: Broken promises*. New York: State University of New York Press.

Erickson, F. (1987). Transformation and school success: The politics and culture of educational achievement. *Anthropology and Education Quarterly, 18*(4), 335–356.

Everhart, R. (1983). *Reading, writing and resistance: Adolescence and labor in a junior high school*. Boston: Routledge and Kegan Paul.

Featherstone, M. (1991). The body in consumer culture. In M. Featherstone, M. Hepworth, & B. Turner (Eds.), *The Body*. London: Sage.

Feher, M. (1987). Of bodies and technologies. In H. Foster (Ed.), *Discussions in contemporary culture*. Seattle: Bay Press.

Felman, S. (1987). *Jacques Lacan and the adventure of insight: Psychoanalysis in contemporary culture*. Cambridge, MA: Harvard University Press.

Ferrell, J. (1995). Urban graffiti: Crime, control and resistance. *Youth and Society, 27*(1), 73–92.

Field, J. and Olafson, L. (1998). Caught in the machine: Resistance, positioning, and pedagogy. *Research in Middle Level Education, 22*(2), 39–55.

Finders, M. (1997). *Just girls: Hidden literacies and life in junior high*. New York: Teachers College Press.

Fine, M. (1991). *Framing drop-outs: Notes on the politics of an urban public high school*. Albany: State University of New York Press.

Fine, M. (1992). Sexuality, schooling, and adolescent females: The missing discourse of desire. In *Disruptive voices: The possibilities of feminist research*. Ann Arbor: University of Michigan Press.

Fontana, A. & Frey, J. (1994). Interviewing. In N. Denzin & Y. Lincoln (Eds.), *Handbook of Qualitative Research*. Thousand Oaks, CA: Sage.

Foucault, M. (1975). *Discipline and punish: The birth of the prison*. (A. Sheridan, Trans.). New York: Vintage. (2nd ed. published 1995)

Foucault, M. (1976). *The history of sexuality. Volume One: Introduction*. (R. Hurley, Trans.). New York: Vintage.

Foucault, M. (1977). *Language, counter-memory, practice: Selected essays and interviews by Michel Foucault*. D. Bouchard (Ed.). Ithaca, NY: Cornell University Press.

Foucault, M. (1980). *Power/Knowledge: Selected interviews and other writings 1972–1977.* C. Gordon (Ed.). (C. Gordon, L. Marshall, J. Mepham, K. Soper, Trans.). New York: Pantheon.

Foucault, M. (1982a). The subject and power. In H. Dreyfus and P. Rabinow (Eds.), *Michel Foucault: Beyond structuralism and hermeneutics.* Chicago: University of Chicago Press.

Foucault, M. (1982b). On the genealogy of ethics. In H. Dreyfus and P. Rabinow (Eds.), *Michel Foucault: Beyond structuralism and hermeneutics.* Chicago: University of Chicago Press.

Foucault, M. (1987). The ethic of care for the self as a practice of freedom. In J. Bernauer and D. Rasmussen (Eds.), *The final Foucault.* Cambridge: The MIT Press.

Gilligan, C. (1982). *In a different voice: Psychological theory and women's development.* Cambridge, MA: Harvard University Press.

Gilligan, C. (1991). Reframing resistance: Women's psychological development. *Women and Therapy, 11,* 5–31.

Gilligan, C., Lyons, P. & Hanmer, T., Eds. (1990). *Making connections: The relational worlds of adolescent girls at Emma Willard School.* Cambridge, MA: Harvard University Press.

Giroux, H. (1983). *Theory and resistance in education: A pedagogy for the opposition.* South Hadley, MA: Bergin and Garvey.

Giroux, H. (1994). Doing cultural studies: Youth and the challenge of pedagogy. *Harvard Educational Review, 64*(3), 278–305.

Gore, J. (1993). *The struggle for pedagogies.* New York: Routledge.

Grosz, E. (1994). *Volatile bodies: Toward a corporeal feminism.* Bloomington: Indiana University Press.

Gupta, A. & Ferguson, J. (1997). Beyond "culture": Space, identity and the politics of difference. In A. Gupta & J. Ferguson (Eds.), *Culture, power, place: Explorations in critical anthropology.* London: Duke University Press.

Haber, H.F. (1996). Foucault pumped: Body politics and the muscled woman. In S. Hekman (Ed.), *Feminist interpretations of Michel Foucault.* University Park, PA: The Pennsylvania State University Press.

Hargreaves, A. (1989). *Curriculum and assessment reform.* Philadelphia, PA: Open University Press.

Hargreaves, A. (1996). Revisiting voice. *Educational Researcher, 1 & 2,* 12–19.

Harper, H. (1997). Disturbing identity and desire: Adolescent girls and wild words. In S. Todd (Ed.), *Learning desire: Perspectives on pedagogy, culture, and the unsaid.* New York: Routledge.

Hartsock, N. (1990). Foucault on power: A theory for feminists? In L. Nicholson (Ed.), *Feminism/Postmodernism.* London: Routledge.

Hekman, S. (1996). Introduction. In S. Hekman (Ed.), *Feminist interpretations of Michel Foucault.* University Park, PA: The Pennsylvania State University Press.

Hepburn, A. (1997). Teachers and secondary school bullying: A postmodern discourse analysis. *Discourse and Society, 8*(1), 27–48.

Hertz, R. (1997). Introduction: Reflexivity and voice. In R. Hertz (Ed.), *Reflexivity and voice.* Thousand Oaks, CA: Sage.

Holstein, J. & Gubrium, J. (1995). *The Active Interview.* Thousand Oaks, CA: Sage.

Jackson, P. (1968). *Life in classrooms.* New York: Holt, Rinehart and Winston.

Jaffee, L. & Lutter, J. (1995). Adolescent girls: Factors influencing low and high body image. *Melpomene Journal, 14*(2), 14–22.

Jaffee, L. & Manzer, R. (1992). Girls' perspectives: Physical activity and self-esteem. *Melpomene Journal, 11*(3), 14–23.

Jardine, D. (1998). *To dwell with a boundless heart: Essays in curriculum theory, hermeneutics and the ecological imagination.* New York: Peter Lang.

Kelly, U. (1997). *Schooling desire: Literacy, cultural politics, and pedagogy.* New York: Routledge.

Kirk, D. (1993). *The body, schooling and culture.* Victoria, Australia: Deakin University Press.

Kirk, D. (1997). Schooling bodies in new times. In J. Fernandez-Balboa (Ed.), *Critical postmodernism in human movement, physical education and sport.* New York: State University of New York Press.

Kohl, H. (1994). *"I won't learn from you": and other thoughts on creative maladjustment.* New York: New Press.

Kvale, S. (1983). The qualitative research interview: A phenomenological and a hermeneutical mode of understanding. *Journal of Phenomenological Psychology, 14*(2), 171–196.

Lesko, N. (1996). Denaturalizing adolescence: The politics of contemporary representations. *Youth and society, 28*(2), 139–161.

Levinson, B. (1998). Discipline seen from below: Student rationales for non-compliance in secondary schools in the United States of America. *Prospects, 28*(4), 601–615.

Lindquist, B. (1994). Beyond student resistance: A pedagogy of possibility. *Teaching Education, 6*(2), 1–8.

Lofland, J. & Lofland, L. (1995). *Analyzing social settings.* Toronto: Wadsworth.

Mahoney, M. (1996). The problem of silence in feminist psychology. *Feminist Studies, 22*(3), 603–625.

Maracek, J. & L. Arcuri (1995). *Talking food, doing gender: The social construction of femininity among sixth-grade girls.* Paper presented at the meeting of American Psychological Association (New York City, NY).

Mason, S. (1999, January 30). Open minds at heart of moral life. *The Calgary Herald*, p. K6.

McLaren, P. (2003). *Life in schools (4th ed.).* New York: Longman.

McRobbie, A. (1980). *Feminism and Youth Culture.* Boston, MA: Unwin Hyman

McRobbie, A. & Garber, J. (1980). Girls and subcultures. In A. McRobbie (Ed.), *Feminism and youth culture.* Boston, MA: Unwin Hyman.

Miron, L.F. & Lauria, M. (1995). Identity politics and student resistance to inner-city public schooling. *Youth and Society, 27*(1), 29–53.

Nicholls, P. (1996). Lessons on lookism. *Reclaiming Children and Youth, 5*(2), 118–122.

Nicholson, L. (1999). *The play of reason.* Ithaca, NY: Cornell University Press.

Nichter, M. & Vuckovic, N. (1994). Fat talk: Body image among adolescent girls. In N. Sault (Ed.), *Many mirrors: Body image and social relations.* New Brunswick, NJ: Rutgers University Press.

Nilges, L. (1998). I thought only fairy tales had supernatural power: A radical feminist analysis of Title IX in physical education. *Journal of Teaching in Physical Education, 17*, 172–194.

Olafson, L. (1996). *Rejecting the docile body: Resisting students and the regime of truth.* Unpublished master's thesis. University of Calgary, Calgary, AB.

Olafson, L., & Field, J. (2003). A moral revisioning of resistance. *The Educational Forum, 67*(2), 140–147.

Olafson, L., & Macintyre Latta, M. (2002). Expecting, accepting, and respecting difference in middle school. *Middle School Journal, 34*(1), 43–47.

O'Reilly, E. (1996). *Physically educating the female body.* Unpublished doctoral dissertation. University of Calgary, Calgary, AB.

Piper, D. (1997). Through the "I" of the teacher: Towards a postmodern conception of self. *McGill Journal of Education, 32*(1), 51–67.

Pipher, M. (1994). *Reviving Ophelia: Saving the selves of adolescent girls.* New York: Ballantine.

Pitt, A.J. (1998). Qualifying resistance: Some comments on methodological dilemmas. *Qualitative Studies in Education, 11*(4), 535–553.

Rampton, B. (1996). Youth, race, and resistance: A sociolinguistic perspective. *Linguistics and Education, 8*, 159–173.

Reinharz, S. (1992). *Feminist methods in social research.* New York: Oxford University Press.

Reinharz, S. (1997). Who am I?: The need for a variety of selves in the field. In R. Hertz (Ed.), *Reflexivity and voice.* Thousand Oaks: Sage.

Roman, L. (1996). Spectacle in the dark: Youth as transgression, display, and repression. *Educational Theory, 46*, 1–22.

Ruiz, R. (1998). Indiscipline or violence: The problem of bullying in school. *Prospects, 28*(4), 587–599.

Sadker, M. & Sadker, D. (1994). *Failing at fairness: How our schools cheat girls.* New York: Simon and Schuster.

Sault, N. (1994). The human mirror. In N. Sault (Ed.), *Many mirrors: Body image and social relations.* New Brunswick, NJ: Rutgers University Press.

Sawicki, J. (1996). Feminism, Foucault and "subjects of power and freedom". In S. Hekman (Ed.), *Feminist interpretations of Michel Foucault.* University Park, PA: The Pennsylvania State University Press.

Sefa Dei, G., Massuca, J., McIsaac, E. & Zine, J. (1997). *Reconstructing "drop-out": A critical ethnography of the dynamics of Black students' disengagement from school.* Toronto: University of Toronto Press.

Seidman, I. (1998). *Interviewing as qualitative research: A guide for researchers in education and the social sciences.* New York: Teachers College Press.

Simmons, R. (2003). *Odd girl out: The hidden culture of aggression in girls.* New York: Harcourt.

Skelton, T. & Valentine, G. (1998). *Cool places: Geographies of youth cultures.* London: Routledge.

Smith, J. K. (1992). Interpretive inquiry: A practical and moral activity. *Theory into Practice, 31*(2), 100–106.

Starr, J. (1981). Adolescents and resistance to schooling: A dialectic. *Youth and Society, 13*(2), 189–227.

Stiggins, R.J. (2001). *Student-involved classroom assessment (3rd ed.).* Upper Saddle River, NJ: Merrill Prentice Hall.

Sun, A. (1995). The development and factor analysis of the student resistance to schooling inventory. *Educational and Psychological Measurement, 55*(5), 841–849.

Taylor, J., Gilligan, C. & Sullivan, A. (1995). *Between voice and silence: Women and girls, race and relationship.* Cambridge, MA: Harvard University Press.

Thorne, B. (1993). *Gender play: Girls and boys in school.* New Brunswick, NJ: Rutgers University Press.

Van Manen, M. (1990). *Researching lived experience: Human science for an action sensitive pedagogy.* London: The Althouse Press.

Vertinsky, P. (1992). Reclaiming space, revisioning body: The quest for gender-sensitive physical education. *Quest, 44*, 373–396.

Walker, M. (1998). *Moral understandings: A feminist study in ethics.* New York: Routledge.

Watkinson, A. (1997). Administrative complicity and systemic violence in education. In J. Epp and A. Watkinson (Eds.), *Systemic violence in education: Broken promises.* New York: State University of New York Press.

Weedon, C. (1987). *Feminist practice and poststructuralist theory.* Oxford: Basil Blackwell.

Willis, P. (1977). *Learning to labour.* Hampshire: Gower Publishing.

Wolf, N. (1990). *The beauty myth.* Toronto: Random House.

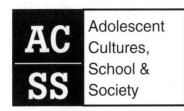

Joseph L. DeVitis & Linda Irwin-DeVitis
GENERAL EDITORS

As schools struggle to redefine and restructure themselves, they need to be cognizant of the new realities of adolescents. Thus, this series of monographs and textbooks is committed to depicting the variety of adolescent cultures that exist in today's post-industrial societies. It is intended to be a primarily qualitative research, practice, and policy series devoted to contextual interpretation and analysis that encompasses a broad range of interdisciplinary critique. In addition, this series will seek to provide a pragmatic, pro-active response to the current backlash of conservatism that continues to dominate political discourse, practice, and policy. This series seeks to address issues of curriculum theory and practice; multicultural education; aggression and violence; the media and arts; school dropouts; homeless and runaway youth; alienated youth; at-risk adolescent populations; family structures and parental involvement; and race, ethnicity, class, and gender studies.

Send proposals and manuscripts to the general editors at:

Joseph L. DeVitis & Linda Irwin-DeVitis
College of Education and Human Development
University of Louisville
Louisville, KY 40292-0001

To order other books in this series, please contact our Customer Service Department at:

(800) 770-LANG (within the U.S.)
(212) 647-7706 (outside the U.S.)
(212) 647-7707 FAX

or browse online by series at:

WWW.PETERLANGUSA.COM

LC1755 .O53 2006

Olafson, Lori,

"It's just easier not to
 go to school" :
        c2006.

2008 11 14

0 1341 1133670 4

RECEIVED

DEC 1 6 2008

GUELPH HUMBER LIBRARY
205 Humber College Blvd
Toronto, ON   M9W 5L7